Cambridge Elements

Elements in Beckett Studies
edited by
Dirk Van Hulle
University of Oxford
Mark Nixon
University of Reading

QUOTIDIAN BECKETT

Art of Everyday Life

Patrick Bixby
Arizona State University

Shaftesbury Road, Cambridge CB2 8EA, United Kingdom

One Liberty Plaza, 20th Floor, New York, NY 10006, USA

477 Williamstown Road, Port Melbourne, VIC 3207, Australia

314–321, 3rd Floor, Plot 3, Splendor Forum, Jasola District Centre, New Delhi – 110025, India

103 Penang Road, #05–06/07, Visioncrest Commercial, Singapore 238467

Cambridge University Press is part of Cambridge University Press & Assessment, a department of the University of Cambridge.

We share the University's mission to contribute to society through the pursuit of education, learning and research at the highest international levels of excellence.

www.cambridge.org
Information on this title: www.cambridge.org/9781009486156

DOI: 10.1017/9781009486118

© Patrick Bixby 2026

This publication is in copyright. Subject to statutory exception and to the provisions of relevant collective licensing agreements, no reproduction of any part may take place without the written permission of Cambridge University Press & Assessment.

When citing this work, please include a reference to the DOI 10.1017/9781009486118

First published 2026

A catalogue record for this publication is available from the British Library

ISBN 978-1-009-48615-6 Hardback
ISBN 978-1-009-48613-2 Paperback
ISSN 2632-0746 (online)
ISSN 2632-0738 (print)

Cambridge University Press & Assessment has no responsibility for the persistence or accuracy of URLs for external or third-party internet websites referred to in this publication and does not guarantee that any content on such websites is, or will remain, accurate or appropriate.

For EU product safety concerns, contact us at Calle de José Abascal, 56, 1°, 28003 Madrid, Spain, or email eugpsr@cambridge.org

Quotidian Beckett

Art of Everyday Life

Elements in Beckett Studies

DOI: 10.1017/9781009486118
First published online: January 2026

Patrick Bixby
Arizona State University
Author for correspondence: Patrick Bixby, patrick.bixby@asu.edu

Abstract: Samuel Beckett was a writer of the everyday. Despite his association with the literary avant-garde and his increasingly spare aesthetic, his writing betrays an enduring preoccupation with the quotidian rhythms of modern life, including the experiences of boredom, routine, habit and consumption. *Quotidian Beckett: Art of Everyday Life* explores the writer's evolving response to this domain of experience, which philosophers and sociologists have paradoxically identified as both everywhere and nowhere, obvious and enigmatic. Drawing on Henri Lefebvre's influential theories of everyday life, the Element also demonstrates how Beckett's writing, by generating forms that resist transparency and closure, invites us to see the mundane in unfamiliar, unsettling and politically charged ways. In this regard, his artistic achievement lies in rendering the elusiveness of the quotidian vivid to a degree that other modes of discourse seldom do.

Keywords: Samuel Beckett, everyday life, late modernism, Henri Lefebvre, materialist criticism

© Patrick Bixby 2026

ISBNs: 9781009486156 (HB), 9781009486132 (PB), 9781009486118 (OC)
ISSNs: 2632-0746 (online), 2632-0738 (print)

Contents

Introduction   1

1 A Form to Accommodate the Quotidian: *Dream of Fair to Middling Women*, *Murphy* and *Watt*   11

2 Almost a Routine, Twice: *Waiting for Godot* and *Endgame*   25

3 Negativity and Happiness: *Happy Days*   37

4 The Terrorism of Everyday Life: *Rough for Theatre II*, *The Lost Ones* and *Rockaby*   48

Conclusion   60

References   65

Introduction

> The sun shone, having no alternative, on the nothing new. Murphy sat out of it, as though he were free, in a mew in West Brompton. Here for what might have been six months he had eaten, drunk, slept, and put his clothes on and off, in a medium-sized cage of north-western aspect commanding an unbroken view of medium-sized cages of south-eastern aspect. Soon he would have to make other arrangements for the mew had been condemned. Soon he would have to buckle to and start eating, drinking, sleeping, and putting his clothes on and off in quite alien surroundings.
> (Beckett, 2009a, 3)

The opening paragraph of Beckett's debut novel, *Murphy* (1938), reveals a writer preoccupied with the quotidian. Its eponymous protagonist lives a life dominated by monotony, by the routines of bodily upkeep that seem automatic and unthinking – repeated day after day, without variation or novelty, as predictably as the sun's regular rounds. The redundancy of Beckett's prose emphasises the redundancy of the protagonist's activity. In his small London flat, Murphy appears to be one of those urban inhabitants trapped, like a prisoner, in a cycle of activity that allows little room for creativity or variety of experience. What is more, the workings of metropolitan capitalism and urban development have imposed themselves on the private sphere of his home, ensuring that these routines will soon be displaced to some other small flat, all too like this one, elsewhere in the city. Based on the evidence provided in the opening lines of the novel, we might begin to sense that something has gone seriously awry and we can start to see an image of acute isolation coming into focus, as new forms of social and economic organisation consume private spaces, while producing a mode of life defined by various forms of privation. We might also begin to perceive a form of alienation resulting from the expansion and pervasiveness of capitalism in an advanced industrialised society, which severs any harmonious connection between the individual and the lived experience of his surroundings. Here, freedom is associated not, or not only, with the philosophical matter of free will but with resistance against the imperative to 'buckle to' his repetitive daily activities in a struggle with prevailing social and economic forces. In short, this will be a novel concerned with how an individual gets through his days in the modern world.

As the narrative continues, however, the remarkable way that Murphy gets through his days promises to reveal the everyday in a different light: 'He sat naked in his rocking-chair of undressed teak, guaranteed not to crack, warp, shrink, corrode, or creak at night' (3). Held in position by seven tightly knotted scarves, Beckett's protagonist perspires as he stares intently, his 'eyes, cold and unwavering as a gull's', at a juncture between the wall and the ceiling of his small apartment, his meditative repose so profound that his 'breath was not perceptible' (3). Suddenly, the ordinary has become quite strange. For Murphy has integrated a novel ritual into his daily routine, one that might evoke sadomasochistic sexuality, self-imposed catatonia, radical quietism, or any number of other idiosyncratic lifestyle choices or mental maladies. We might see this as an image, perhaps even the clearest image, of the modernist retreat into private subjectivity and psychopathology in response to the alienating conditions of modernity, as Georg Lukács later did in his infamous condemnation of Beckett (along with other modernists such as Joyce, Kafka and Musil). Indeed, a prominent strain of modernist criticism would go on to read these depictions of isolated men trapped in their rooms as images of existentialist despair or a metaphysical rupture between the self and the world. But this is too facile. Given the playful presentation of his protagonist, Beckett could just as soon be accused of parodying any presumed modernist impulse to withdraw from the everyday. This sense is only compounded by the fact that Murphy is abruptly roused from his reverie: 'Somewhere a cuckoo-clock, having struck between twenty and thirty, became the echo of a street-cry, which now entering the mew gave *Quid pro quo! Quid pro quo!* directly' (3). There is no easy escape from the realm of social and economic exchange and its hold on everyday life in capitalist society, which stubbornly exert their alienating influences on private consciousness.

As we will see in the pages to come, Beckett's art is deeply engaged with the everyday, albeit in modes very different from the social realism favoured by Lukács. Rather, even as his work sheds historical details and becomes increasingly (though never entirely) abstract over the course of a six-decades-long career, Beckett's engagement with the quotidian consistently explores both formal and thematic means to make the familiar strange, the ordinary extraordinary, often placing its most recognisable attributes in 'quite alien surroundings' (5). Perhaps paradoxically, this process does not strip his work of historicity. The gradually more insistent elisions and negations, the abandoning of social contexts and cultural specificities, make visible some of the defining contradictions (and, often, the vexing limitations) of everyday life in the modern world, which tend to be disguised or disregarded by more conventional means of representation.

Despite Beckett's early and abiding interest in the quotidian, his work has seldom been discussed in relation to everyday life or the work of his contemporary, the most prominent theorist of everyday life in the twentieth century, Henri Lefebvre. Although Lefebvre was born in France, his long career stretched alongside Beckett's from studies in Paris in the 1920s and early efforts at publication in the 1930s, through the tumult of the war years, resistance to the pervasive influence of Existentialism, an extended reckoning with post-war

French society and post-Holocaust European civilisation in the 1940s and 1950s, a rise to prominence and an association with the emergence of postmodernism in the 1960s and 1970s, and continued productivity through the 1980s. For much of this time, the two inhabited the same intellectual milieu in Paris. Despite their different allegiances, their writings express a shared antagonism towards the bureaucratic control and regulated consumption of post-war French society and late capitalist societies more generally. In this context, both refined modes of writing that investigate the everyday as a domain where habit, repetition and mundane activities take precedence over the natural, the divine, or the mythological. Both provide us with a sense that the everyday is not simply a background against which significant events take place but rather the very setting in which individuals negotiate their desires and identities. More than any other thinker of Beckett's generation, Lefebvre attempted to refute the distinctions between the philosophical and the non-philosophical, turning away from the ostensibly serious 'notions of Being, Depth and Substance' and towards the seemingly trivial matters and mundane activities (Lefebvre, 1971, 14). Rather than critiquing everyday life in the name of grander truths and thus risking his own ideological contradictions, he sought to critique the mundane on its own terms. Now that critics have started to address Beckett's writing in relation to what Mark Nixon calls 'the essentially quotidian nature of human existence', it becomes imperative to bring Lefebvre's work into the conversation, in order to better assess the critical, sometimes even antithetical, force of Beckett's attention to the everyday (Nixon, 2019, 1).[1]

Reading Beckett this way means attending to the base matters of his writing, relating to quotidian concerns about shelter, rest, labour, food and the function of common objects and familiar commodities. Lukács's condemnation of Beckett hinged on his depiction of a world where there seems to be no possibility of alleviating the damaging social, political and economic conditions that attended the emergence of modernism as a cultural form. This appraisal identifies the only solution offered in his writing as a pathological withdrawal, à la Murphy and many of his other protagonists, into alienated subjectivity. This withdrawal is mimicked on the level of form by the increasing abstraction of Beckett's work and its perceived movement away from the material world and its social circumstances. Theodor Adorno would famously defend Beckett

---

[1] See, for example, the special issue 'Never Neglect the Small Things: Beckett and the Everyday' of the *Journal of Beckett Studies* (Nixon and Van Hulle, 2019) and the chapter 'Beckett, War and the Everyday' in Will Davies' *Samuel Beckett and the Second World War: Politics, Propaganda, and a 'Universal Become Provisional'* (2020). These contributions were preceded by important studies of Beckett's 'material imagination', including Steven Connor's *Beckett, Modernism, and the Material Imagination* (2014) and Julie Bates's *Beckett's Art of Salvage: Writing and Material Imagination, 1932–1987* (2017).

against this evaluation by stressing the ways that his isolated figures seem to invoke a transformation in his readers, and the formal qualities of his works, as James McNaughton puts it, 'undermine[] hypostasizing and ahistorical philosophical abstractions by making literal and physical the aftereffects of calamity' (McNaughton, 2018, 82). Meanwhile, in his passing comments on Beckett's work, Lefebvre would largely repeat the then reigning critical orthodoxy, which framed it as the artful expression of an Existentialist fascination with the sordid and marginal elements of modern life. But, as we shall see, he also contributed to this debate in ways that maintained the critical capacity of modern art to intervene in the transformation of the modern world. With the aid of Lefebvre's theories and those thinkers who responded to them (including Maurice Blanchot and Michel de Certeau), an emphasis on the everyday in Beckett's work – including its tendency to isolate individuals, abstract details and thwart meaning – can help us to access new historical, political *and* aesthetic dimensions of his art, ones that have generally stayed closed even after the historical and political turn in Beckett studies over the last three decades.[2] This will mean returning to the Lukács and Adorno debate over the political significance of Beckett's writing and reviving the (still not settled) question of his relationship with Existentialism, as it relates to quotidian experience. Or, to conceive of the project of this Element in different terms, it means thinking and feeling the everyday with Beckett and Lefebvre to illuminate aspects of quotidian experience that otherwise remain obscured, including the very capacity of the everyday to escape conventional representations and disrupt totalising narratives.

The project of this Element begins with approaching the question of how to define the quotidian. To be sure, this is a notoriously difficult question for the study of everyday life across a range of disciplines and discourses, though in a sense nothing could be more obvious: everyday life is the compendium of daily activities and affects, in all their banality, repetitiveness and concreteness, before they have been transcribed into abstractions. It is the sum total of how most people live most of their lives, though it somehow remains largely beyond their notice, reflection, or comprehension. The quotidian surrounds us on all sides, so that we are always to some extent within it, and even our most elevated activities cannot be entirely detached from it. Yet it remains elusive. For Lefebvre,

---

[2] This turn became apparent with the groundbreaking postcolonial readings of Beckett's oeuvre beginning in the 1990s and reached significant milestones with the publication of Emilie Morin's *Beckett's Political Imagination* (2017) and James McNaughton's *Samuel Beckett and the Politics of Aftermath* (2018), which position his work more clearly in relation to war, fascism and genocide.

> The quotidian is what is humble and solid, what is taken for granted and that of which all the parts follow each other in such a regular, unvarying succession that those concerned have no call to question their sequence; thus it is undated and (apparently) insignificant; though it occupies and preoccupies it is practically untellable, and it is the ethics underlying routine and the aesthetics of familiar settings. At this point it encounters the modern. This word stands for what is novel, brilliant, paradoxical and bears the imprint of technicality and worldliness, it is (apparently) daring and transitory, proclaims its initiative and is acclaimed for it. (Lefebvre, 1971, 24)

Extending Marxist inquiry beyond economic exploitation, Lefebvre makes everyday life central to the theorisation of both modernity and alienation. In its implementation of technology, bureaucracy and other forms of instrumental rationality, modernity has promised to fundamentally improve our social relations – but has failed to do so. Instead, bourgeois society has only become increasingly privatised, individualised and specialised, with a widening separation between private consciousness and social consciousness. For it is at the level of everyday life – like Murphy, immersed in its deficiency, redundancy and mundanity – that the pervasive alienation of modern individuals takes hold through the loss of meaningful engagement with the world and with their own lived experience. But crucially, for Lefebvre, everyday life also possesses the resources for a dialectical negotiation with or a working through of this alienation.

A brief genealogy of the term 'everyday life' (and the terms that have contributed to it, such as *Alltäglichkeit* and *gewöhnliches Leben* in German and *la vie quotidienne* in French) will help us to understand how Lefebvre initiates his inquiry, which evolved significantly over the course of his massive three-volume study *The Critique of Everyday Life* (*Critique de la vie quotidienne*, 1947, 1961, 1981).[3] His extensive theorisation of the everyday follows on from the early work of Lukács, who first articulated his concept of everyday or 'ordinary' life in the essay 'Metaphysik der Tragödie' (1911).[4] In his initial anti-empiricist, pre-Marxist phase, the Hungarian theorist criticised everyday life in a manner that contrasts sharply with his later condemnation of modernism for retreating from the alienating conditions of modernity. For the young Lukács, the everyday was the domain of the merely empirical, the merely superficial, where human existence is detached from 'ultimate questions and ultimate answers' (Lukács, 1974, 155). It was, moreover, a domain of pure contingency, where we are 'entangled by a thousand threads in a thousand accidental bonds and relationships' (157). Here, individuals lead lives

---

[3] This Element cites from the one-volume edition, see Lefebvre (2002).
[4] Citations in this Element are from an English translation, see Lukács (1974).

characterised by emptiness, lives that carry them only to an abiding sense of separation from their own essence and from the world around them. Lukács contrasts this with the realm of tragedy, where humans have shed their daily distractions and their associated inauthenticity to bravely face destiny in the 'harsh mountain air' of their heightened awareness (155). His romantic rejection of the merely empirical thus assigns modern tragedy the task of giving artistic form to 'real' or 'authentic' life, which becomes manifest in the progress of its narratives. All ordinary human relationships fade; all the subtle connections between individuals and objects disappear. In this way, the realm of tragedy presents a vision of human life as timeless and static, transcending the plane of temporal experience and rejecting the trivial necessities, mundane distractions and relentless contingencies of everyday life in favour of a genuinely meaningful existence.

Martin Heidegger, who was familiar with Lukács's early writings, assigned a central role to the concept of *Alltäglichkeit* ('everydayness') in his *Being and Time* ([1927] 1962), using it as a starting point for understanding *Dasein*, the experience of Being specific to human beings. His initial hypothesis is that *Dasein* should be most readily accessible to inquiry in its most ordinary and enduring situation, its 'average everydayness', where it will also exhibit its most essential features. Everydayness is thus conceived as a sort of base condition. But Heidegger also associates everydayness with inauthenticity because it is defined by social conventions, shared beliefs and common rituals. In this everyday state of inauthenticity, *Dasein* succumbs to the projects imposed on it by the 'They' ('das Man'):

> We take pleasure and enjoy ourselves as they take pleasure; we read, see, and judge about literature and art as they see and judge [...] we find 'shocking' what they find shocking. The 'They', which is nothing definite, and which all are, though not as the sum, prescribes the kind of Being of everydayness. (Heidegger, 1962, 164)

Dasein falls *away* from itself as an authentic potentiality and falls *into* the world to the extent that the Being of 'the Others' becomes a dictatorial influence, obscuring or concealing any genuine understanding of the world, albeit in mostly unnoticed ways. For instance, the world-concealing power of the everyday is manifest in what Heidegger calls 'idle talk', which generates endless statements about events in the world, while failing to penetrate their surface and reveal their relevance. Heidegger shares with many of the Existentialists who followed him this sense that quotidian experience, with its mundane concerns and standardised ways of acting, thinking and speaking, separates individuals from themselves and from any authentic connection to the world around them.

Yet, despite this world-concealing power, everydayness is nonetheless fundamental to the self-understanding of *Dasein* because all 'genuine understanding, interpreting and communication, rediscovery and new appropriation come about in it, out of it, and against it' (Heidegger, 1962, 213). Everydayness thus possesses a paradoxical quality in Heidegger's philosophy, for it both conceals *and* reveals *Dasein's* relationship to the world, both presents a domain of conformity and inauthenticity *and* offers an arena of possible means for understanding ourselves and achieving an authentic mode of Being.

While Lefebvre expressed a variety of positions on Heidegger during his long career, many of them decidedly negative, it is undeniable that the two thinkers shared a sense of the importance, both philosophical and sociological, of the everyday. For Lefebvre, however, everyday life cannot be reduced to the conformity and inauthenticity of *Alltäglichkeit* that Lukács and Heidegger emphasise in their writings. In addition to their philosophical contempt for the quotidian, Lefebvre also criticised the theoretical abstractions of Heidegger and other philosophers because they did not adequately capture the rich concreteness of everyday life. Although he viewed the quotidian as the sum of repetitive daily activities, he continually stressed that it is more than simply what escapes philosophical abstraction and other forms of myth-making. Rather, it is a storehouse of marvels and mysteries. At times, it appears that Lefebvre finds an ally in Heidegger to the degree that they both place significance on the social norms, collective rituals and banal language that contribute to everydayness. While Lefebvre does not associate these concerns with inauthenticity per se, he does see them as implicated in alienation, which draws individuals away from their essential humanity or species-being. Like inauthenticity for Lukács and Heidegger, alienation for Lefebvre designates a negative or pejorative facet of everyday life. His conception of alienation derives from the early writings of Marx but ranges far beyond the original focus on the workplace and the marketplace to incorporate the broader spectrum of everyday life under capitalism. It comes to designate a withdrawal from the public sphere and political participation under the conditions of late capitalism, including widespread consumerism and pervasive bureaucratic control. Disalienation, on the other hand, means the transformation of everyday life by locating the extraordinary in the all too ordinary, promoting opportunities for creative and communal activity and healing the rift between the private and the public.

In pursuing the significance of the everyday, Lefebvre often stresses recurrence, the redundant activities of labour and leisure, the redundant movement of hours, days, weeks and so on – what he calls 'the great problem of repetition' (Lefebvre, 1987, 10). Indeed, the French *quotidien*, even more than the English 'everyday', emphasises this sense of repetition, of the coming back day after day, of that which is done on a regular basis. This emphasis points to the fact that some form of everyday life has always existed, even if its forms were very different in previous eras when the cyclical repetition of days and nights, seasons and harvests, life and death predominated. In modern life, these natural cycles succumb to a constant monotony in which each day looks very much like the next, even when the location changes: eating, drinking, sleeping, putting clothes on and off in one 'medium-sized cage' or another. Everyday life becomes total quotidian-ness, but unremarked and forgotten almost instantly (except, perhaps, when an effort is made to render it into art). According to Lefebvre, the failure of philosophy to account for the everyday can be attributed in large part to its focus on the 'exceptional moment' as an object of inquiry, which in turn provides a fixed perspective and distances its analysis from the rhythms of everyday life. It is crucial for him, nonetheless, that examination of the everyday places a critical distance between the investigator and the object of investigation in order to abandon the passivity and conformity of living the everyday. Yet, as Blanchot was to argue in his oft-cited review of *The Critique of Everyday Life, Volume 2*, efforts to apprehend the everyday must also come to terms with a certain negativity, with what 'escapes', with what threatens to undermine any effort to make it signify or integrate it with a totalising narrative (Blanchot, 1987, 12–20). It is perhaps no surprise, then, that Lefebvre's analysis of the everyday often turns towards literature and its capacity to mediate the quotidian, not just through the representation of the mundane details of everyday life but through a tropology that integrates itself with quotidian-ness and yet resists describing it plainly or naming it directly.

Beckett's literary engagement with the everyday begins even before his first published novel, with his first book, *Proust*, which also opens with reflections on repetition, habit and the vexations of the quotidian as they relate to *À la recherche du temps perdu*. The idiosyncratic essay ultimately tells us far more about Beckett's own preoccupations as he began his writing career than it does about the nature of Proust's achievement. The Irish writer would later lament that his commentary was 'too abstract', relying heavily, as it does, on his recent reading of Schopenhauer's *The World as Will and Representation*, but it still bears closely on the problem of everydayness and its role in constituting both the subject and the object:

> There is no escape from the hours and the days. Neither from tomorrow nor from yesterday. There is no escape from yesterday because yesterday has deformed us, or been deformed by us. The mood is of no importance.

Deformation has taken place. Yesterday is not a milestone that has been passed, but a daystone on the beaten track of the years, and irremediably part of us, within us, heavy and dangerous. We are not merely more weary because of yesterday, we are other, no longer what we were before the calamity of yesterday. A calamitous day, but calamitous not necessarily in content. The good or evil disposition of the object has neither reality nor significance. The immediate joys and sorrows of the body and the intelligence are so many superfoetations. Such as it was, it has been assimilated to the only world that has reality and significance, the world of our own latent consciousness, and its cosmography has suffered a dislocation. (Beckett, 1957, 3)

At the outset of his study, Beckett asserts that the everyday may be forgettable and often forgotten in our conscious experience, and yet it is deeply inscribed in our unconscious and, as he will argue when turning to Proust, prone to return to us through involuntary memory. We thus live with the weight of the everyday and its inescapable temporality, which continually burdens the individual, so that our internal map of meaning is incessantly shaped and reshaped by quotidian experience. Like Lefebvre, Beckett emphasises 'the great problem of repetition', the redundant movement of hours and days that make up quotidian experience, as well as the seemingly unremarkable quality of such experience that nonetheless leaves its mark on the individual (Lefebvre, 1987, 10). He also suggests the inescapable influence of the quotidian in the various calamities, both subjective and objective, of any given day. But, unlike Lefebvre, Beckett stresses the deforming effects of these accumulated calamities, these daily repetitions, which are disregarded by most and which thus fail to enhance their self-understanding. The quotidian, that is, lulls us into a kind of numbness, from which Proust would have us awaken through heightened forms of perception and reflection, piercing through the mundane to some deeper reality (even if Beckett registers his doubts about this possibility).

This opening exposition sets the stage for Beckett's reflections on habit, which he defines as 'a compromise effected between the individual and his environment, or between the individual and his own organic eccentricities, the guarantee of a dull inviolability, the lightning-conductor of his existence'. He continues:

Habit is the ballast that chains the dog to his vomit. Breathing is habit. Life is habit. [...] Habit then is the generic term for the countless treaties concluded between the countless subjects that constitute the individual and their countless correlative objects. (Beckett, 1957, 8)

In her influential essay 'The Invention of the Everyday', Rita Felski has denounced these reflections as typifying a modernist disdain for the everyday, which 'has exposed these congealed patterns of daily life and questioned the sleepwalking demeanour inspired by the tyranny of habit' (Felski, 2000, 90).[5] But this is to overstate Beckett's claims. Borrowing from Schopenhauer, the young writer arrives at a position that parallels Heidegger's in several respects. The ordinary everydayness of *Dasein* incorporates habituated patterns of speech and behaviour that work to distract the individual from Being as such by dissolving *Dasein* into a form of self-forgetfulness. But where Heidegger's emphasis falls on inauthenticity, as generalised ways of thinking and acting are incorporated into the self, Beckett's attention focuses on how certain settled ways of engaging with the world both provide a kind of continuity to the self and work to accommodate the self to its everyday surroundings. In this regard, habit is a necessary compromise between the self and the domain of contingency in which it lives, and thus habit protects the self from the calamities that, for Schopenhauer, make up the content of daily life, even though this protection slips away from time to time:

> The periods of transition that separate consecutive adaptations [...] represent the perilous zones in the life of the individual, dangerous, precarious, painful, mysterious, and fertile, when for a moment the boredom of living is replaced by the suffering of being. (Beckett, 1957, 8)

But habit, as a means of stabilising the ego and its relations with being, necessarily fails to bridge the gap from one stage of life to the next, amid an unstable world of multiplicity.

Most importantly for Beckett, then, habit functions to deaden our perceptions and anaesthetise us from 'the suffering of being: that is, the free play of every faculty'. Habit is the mode of activity most closely associated with the everyday, for it manifests in the unvarying succession of behaviours that proceed without reflection, at least as long as the setting remains familiar:

> Because the pernicious devotion of habit paralyses our attention, drugs those handmaidens of perception whose co-operation is not absolutely essential. Habit is like Francoise, the immortal cook of the Proust household, who knows what has to be done, and will slave all day and all night rather than tolerate any redundant activity in the kitchen. But our current habit of living is as incapable of dealing with the mystery of a strange sky or a strange room, with any circumstance unforeseen in her curriculum. (Beckett, 1957, 9)

---

[5] In *Modernism and the Ordinary*, Liesl Olson provides a more nuanced account of the role that Proust and Beckett, 'especially as Proust's work is *read* by Beckett', played 'in defining the primacy of the ordinary during the modernist period', but she also focuses on 'Beckett's disdain for the everyday' in a way that neglects much of his oeuvre (Olson, 2014, 37; emphasis in original).

As we shall see, this is a particularly important insight for Beckett's own career as a writer. The unexpected or unfamiliar new context confounds habit and thus shakes us out of the deadening routines that keep distress at bay. Unable to manage the sheer multiplicity of being, we fall back on habit to make sense of things and to replace the 'suffering of being' with the 'boredom of living'. According to Beckett, again following Schopenhauer, our habits of perception work to hide the inner essence of objects in the cloud of conceptions and preconceptions that we impose upon the world. In his reading, the narrator of *À la recherche du temps perdu* oscillates between these two states as his habits numb him to the experiences he prizes, until they give way and a deluge of involuntary memories is allowed to flow into his consciousness. Proust's contribution to the literature of the everyday thus exists largely in his exploration of our habits of perception, perhaps especially the difficulty of transforming these habits: 'an operation described by Proust as "longer and more difficult than the turning inside out of an eyelid, and which consists in the imposition of our own familiar soul on the terrifying soul of our surroundings"' (26). But crucially for Beckett, his writing also demonstrates how art can draw attention to the everyday in ways that allow for contemplation and critique, for seeing the ordinary in extraordinary ways, rather than merely dismissing or denying it.

1 A Form to Accommodate the Quotidian: *Dream of Fair to Middling Women*, *Murphy* and *Watt*

As has often been noted, Beckett's career as a novelist began in dialogue with both Proust and Joyce, those two giants of modernist literature, those two great chroniclers of the everyday, as the young author sought a form appropriate to accommodate the 'mess' of quotidian experience. For Lefebvre, Joyce's *Ulysses* is particularly significant because it 'rescues, one after the other, each facet of the quotidian from anonymity', not just by cataloguing the 'manner in which ordinary men and women spent that day, their occupations, preoccupations, labours or leisure', but by artfully weaving together 'the different levels of meaning, familiar, historical, kindred, foreign and so forth', that make up the everyday (Lefebvre, 1971, 1–2). The orchestral arrangements of *Ulysses* manage to capture both the polyphony of everyday speech and the proliferations of everyday life. In a sense, the loose, uneven, nearly incoherent form of Beckett's first attempt at a novel, *Dream of Fair to Middling Women* – which collects fragments written in different voices, styles and registers – might seem entirely apposite to the amorphous quality of the everyday. But, unlike *Ulysses*, *Dream* abandons any attempt to reassemble these fragments into some elaborate architecture or grand synthesis in favour of a kind of entropic deformation of the genre, which turns its linguistic energies towards disruption and disfiguration, rather than towards the mastery of literary form. In this way, the novel also initiates a series of attempts to come to terms with the quotidian in Beckett's subsequent novels *Murphy* and *Watt*, which present everyday life as both an inhospitable environment for their alienated protagonists and a domain of experience that largely resists signification through conventional means.

Beckett's initial effort to deform the novel form radically (and often sardonically) refuses more familiar approaches to narration and characterisation that impose some recognisable order on the fictional world by appealing to established literary modes of sense-making. In fact, this refusal is repeatedly made explicit in the novel through the narrator's repeated attacks on the 'whipped verisimilitude' of novelists such as Austen and Balzac, whom he accuses of falsifying human experience by imposing an artificial coherence on their fictional worlds and affirming certain assumptions about social reality in the process (Beckett, 1993, 118). He also mocks the social realism of Dickens by associating his own hyperbolic rhetoric with that of the British author after a particularly exaggerated paragraph: '(Overstatement. Dickens.)' (159). No doubt, as Lefebvre acknowledges, Joyce's fiction had already opposed anything like the stereotypical protagonists and convention plots of his novelistic forebears, including those who had given ample attention to the details of quotidian experience. And yet Beckett's novel goes one step further by rejecting the masterful orchestrations and symbolic systems of his Irish predecessor, radically problematising the rescue and representation of everyday life. At the same time, in retaining a playful Joycean quality in its prose and engaging in the overt mockery of novelistic conventions, *Dream* allows a parodic variety of social critique to emerge.

Amid the structural deformations and the discursive eclecticism that characterise *Dream*, perhaps the most evident feature of the everyday is quotidian speech, the idle talk of the street corner, the public house, or the social gathering. The banal, though sometimes heated language of these familiar settings paints a verbal portrait of everyday life in 1930s Dublin, where various voices chatter on about this and that, about nothing in particular. In the penultimate section of the novel, for instance, Beckett presents us with a party scene reminiscent of Joyce's 'The Dead', though this gathering is attended by a far more diverse range of guests, who generate a cacophony of conversations in an overcrowded home on the edge of the city. The interlocutors include a number of generic figures, identified as 'the Student', 'the Poet' and so on, as well as a far more particular and peculiar group:

> a Gael, an Irish one, then the Shawly with her Chas [...] the Polar Bear [...] the Countess of Parabimbi [...] Miss Frica [...] Pansy [...] Lilly Neary,

> Olga, Miriam, Alga, Ariana, tall Tib, slender Sib, Katty, Alba [...]. Two novelists, a bibliomaniac and his mistress, a paleographer, a violist d'amore with his instrument in a bag, a popular parodist with his sister and six daughters, a still more popular professor of Bullscrit and Comparative Ovoidology, the macaco the worse for drink, an incontinent native speaker, a prostrated arithmomaniac, a communist decorator just back from the Moscow reserves, a merchant, two grave Jews, a rising whore, three more poets with Lauras to match, a disaffected cicisbeo, the inevitable envoy of the Fourth Estate, a phalanx of Grafton Street Stürmers and Jem Higgins. (Beckett, 1993, 217)

The conversation, characterised by intellectual pretension and general miscommunication, begins with an exchange between Chas and the Student, who demands 'without exordium' of the former: 'In what sense [...] did you use *sense* when you said...' (217). From there, the various exchanges devolve from standard greetings, practical questions and trivial remarks to discord, misunderstanding and insult, which do not so much mimic conventional small talk as parodically heighten it, so that the superficiality of everyday speech reaches a kind of apogee: '"To my mind" boomed presumptuously the ovoidologist "the greatest triumph of human thought was the calculation of Neptune from the observed vagaries of the orbit of Uranus." "And yours," said the P.B.' (221–2). In these exchanges, Beckett provides us a glimpse of what was to come in his iconic post-war dramas, which offer less a faithful representation of 'everyday speech' than a humorous send-up of such language, the dialogue of his characters becoming a means to caricature and critique this region of discourse. Such exaggerated small talk only emphasises the dissatisfactions of the social environment and the emptiness of everyday speech as a mode of communication that fails, despite its pretensions, to break through the surface of whatever subject the characters broach or indeed to penetrate the deepseated banality of their quotidian experience. In this regard, *Dream* can be read as a satire of Irish society during a sustained phase of cultural and political dissonance that has permeated the daily lives of its citizens.

But what is most remarkable about Beckett's first novel in this regard are the recurring efforts of its protagonist, Belacqua Shuah, to escape from the discord of quotidian existence into the 'wombtomb' of his own mind. If the novel as a form has been seen to accommodate subjective experience to objective necessity through narratives of personal formation and social integration, however tenuous these processes might be, *Dream* traces an opposing trajectory towards isolation and solipsism. But it is here, in his self-fashioned realm of solipsistic withdrawal, that Belacqua believes he has arrived at something more authentic than the superficial distractions of everyday life:

> Torture by thought and trial by living, because it was fake thought and false living, stayed outside the tunnel. But in the umbra, the tunnel, when the mind went wombtomb, then it was real thought and real living, living thought. Thought not skivvying for living nor living chivvying thought up to the six-and-eightpenny conviction, but live cerebration that drew no wages and emptied no slops. (Beckett, 1993, 45)

These descriptions with their overwrought prose are a source of irony, since Belacqua's inner world proves every bit as unsatisfactory as the outer world. Moreover, his habit of retreat and his repeated attempts to suspend his will prove incapable of protecting him from the suffering manifest in sexual desire, romantic frustration and social disappointment. Belacqua seeks escape from this bombardment behind a mental 'earthworks': 'this to break not so much the flow of people and things to him as the ebb of him to people and things' (Beckett, 1993, 43). But, as a strategy for coping with the relations of everyday life, both social and economic, his withdrawal proves largely unsatisfactory and provides much of the biting humour of *Dream*. Beckett's first novel thus comically accentuates, even literalises, the attention to interiority in its high modernist precursors, including *À la recherche du temps perdu* (i.e., *monologue intérieur*) and *Ulysses* (i.e., stream of consciousness) and in the process highlights the frailty of the individual in relation to the forces of their social world. Further, in Belacqua's repeated failures to withdraw, and in the abiding irony of his situation, the novel demonstrates to the reader that the protagonist's desire for isolation is indeed a form of alienation – that is, socially mediated and fundamentally historical in character, rather than some unchanging, inevitable, or existential condition.

The concept of the wombtomb, this space set aside from the everyday, owes something to Beckett's reading of Schopenhauer's philosophy (as well as his modernist predecessors) insofar as it represents a space of habitual retreat from quotidian experience. Belacqua shares in the idea, articulated in 'The Metaphysics of Sexual Love' in Volume Two of *The World as Will and Representation*, that romantic love and sexual attraction represent the greatest threats to the suppression of the will and the avoidance of suffering. His efforts to enter the wombtomb repeatedly capitulate to the myriad distractions of both everyday life and sexual desire:

> He trained his little brain to hold its breath, he made covenants of all kinds with his senses, he forced the lids of the little brain down against the flaring bric-a-brac, in every imaginable way he flogged on his coenesthesis to enwomb him, to exclude the bric-a-brac and expunge his consciousness. (Beckett, 1993, 123)

But, in the end, it is 'All for nothing'. Beckett's first novel seems to affirm *avant la lettre* the criticism that Lukács levelled against his famous mid-career prose and other prominent examples of literary modernism for endorsing a retreat from the sordid conditions of everyday life into private consciousness and even psychopathology. Admittedly, the trope of the wombtomb, with its suggestion of a symbolic reintegration with the maternal body and a corresponding flirtation with the death drive, would seem more amenable to the concerns of psychoanalysis than to those of a materialist or historicist criticism. But the space of the wombtomb invites us to consider the failings of both Beckett's protagonist and the everyday world around him, and, indeed, to see those failings even more clearly in relation to the strange interior realm of his private consciousness. In this regard, we might see *Dream* as announcing Beckett's career-long preoccupation not only with the tension between private consciousness and the public sphere but with the relationship between persistent alienation and everyday life.

To be sure, this relationship is a principal concern of Beckett's next attempt at a novel. *Murphy* can be said to parody repeatedly the modernist obsession with the inner workings of the mind, nowhere more explicitly and risibly than in its anomalous chapter six, where the narrator describes his eponymous protagonist's interiority in meticulous detail:

> Murphy's mind pictured itself as a large hollow sphere, hermetically closed to the universe without [...] the mental experience was cut off from the physical experience, the agreement of part of its content with physical fact did not confer worth on that part (Beckett, 2009a, 70)

Perhaps more than anything else, building on the image of Belacqua's wombtomb in *Dream*, the chapter pokes fun at the fantasies of a would-be solipsist as it reveals how Murphy's mind pictures *itself* to be. By virtue of its detachment from outer reality, this image of his mind also serves what we might call – following Michel Foucault – a heterotopian function, emphasising the radically different quality of his inner realm, with its own rules and principles, in contrast to the broader world that lies beyond its confines. This parody of Cartesianism becomes a picture of radical alienation, as well as a judgement on everyday life in the modern world and the ways that it has degraded and deformed the human subject. The chapter suggests that Murphy can only attain the freedom he seeks by withdrawing fully from the 'big world' of social reality into the 'little world' of private consciousness: in the first two 'zones of his private world Murphy felt sovereign and free, in the one to requite himself, in the other to move as he pleased from one unparalleled beatitude to another', and in the third 'he was not free, but a mote in the dark of absolute freedom' (72). However, to see the chapter as evidence that Beckett's art endorses a pessimistic retreat from the everyday world into isolation and despair is to completely miss the irony of the novel: Murphy's idea of self-sufficiency is revealed as little more than a desperate means of self-defence. If his predilection for solipsism is a decisive judgement on social reality, it is also a misguided impulse that drives him to increasingly desperate escape attempts and ultimately, if indirectly, to his untimely death.

The narrative that leads to this conclusion does not privilege this image of solipsistic and pathological withdrawal at the expense of broader social realities or historical conditions. In many ways, compared to the earlier *Dream*, *Murphy* is a rather conventional novel, situating its protagonist and his mind within a familiar assemblage of social institutions and even offering us a recognisable variety of social analysis. The narrative is perhaps best viewed as a late modernist response to the nineteenth-century realist novel of the city by Balzac or Dickens, even more than to the high modernist novel of the city by Joyce or Woolf, which had recently offered readers new ways of coming to terms with the intensification of urban life that had become everyday experience for more and more modern individuals.[6] The novel genre, particularly in its social realist manifestations, is the literary form most closely associated with the treatment of everyday experience because its verisimilitude relied in large part on the depiction of the common, the ordinary, the familiar. In its capacious form, which nonetheless retained a loose structure, the novel could accommodate the proliferating details that make up everyday life as it sought to fill in the background of its narrative setting and recover the dross of the modern world from anonymity and obscurity. This capacity was an important facet of the complex representation of the relationship between the individual and society as a whole, which Lukács and many other Marxist critics saw as the central task of the novel genre. But there is clearly a tension between the form of the novel, as capacious as it is, and the proliferation of common things that make up the everyday, a tension that suggests the problem of representing the everyday as such, of tracking down its significant details, of extracting them from the teeming background of information.[7]

The experimental elements of *Murphy*, as muted as they are, throw suspicion on the normalisation of everyday experience as somehow self-evident and ideologically unproblematic that social realism and the novel

---

[6] On the representation of the everyday in *Ulysses* and *Mrs. Dalloway*, see Olson (2014, 33–88).
[7] For recent perspectives on the relationship between the novel form and everyday life, see Cogle et al. (2018) and Langbauer (2019).

form more generally had helped to promote in previous generations. Beckett's novel calls attention to the problem of representing the everyday with a series of playful rhetorical moves: not just the extended reflections on the mind of its protagonist but the prosaic list of physical traits attributed to his love interest, Celia, the academic cross-referencing of details from one section of the novel to the next, and, overseeing all of this, an omniscient narrator who is nonetheless self-conscious about the failings of his narrative. In this way, *Murphy* also raises questions about the status of everyday life and the capacity of any form to adequately accommodate it. It alerts us to the eccentric politics that characterise much of Beckett's oeuvre and its abiding preoccupation with the tensions between the 'flaring bric-a-brac' of quotidian experience and the fading autonomy of consciousness, which does not bolster the myth of human solitude so much as implicate it in the concerns of quotidian experience. In doing so, *Murphy* performs an inquiry into the alienating forces of everyday life that have led its protagonist to pursue 'his Belacqua fantasy' of withdrawal from social and economic intercourse, which belonged to those fantasies 'that lay just beyond the frontiers of suffering, it was the first landscape of freedom' (Beckett, 2009a, 51). As it subtly and, at times, not so subtly undermines the conventions of realist fiction, the novel still positions itself for confrontation with the alienating qualities of everyday experience, by highlighting the contradictions and failures of the society that has driven Murphy to his radical quietism.

This is perhaps most evident in the way *Murphy* presents urban experience and the social production of urban space in Depression-era London. Indeed, the novel participates in a tradition of examining the modern city as a site where individuals feel alienated from each other and where the effects of capitalism and commodification have impressed themselves deeply on their lives. Lefebvre would introduce the notion of spatial alienation in his 1974 book *La Production de l'espace* (*The Production of Space*) to emphasise the ways that the built environment, especially in urban settings, has come to serve the goals of profit and efficiency instead of the human needs of connection and community. *Murphy* addresses these concerns in a scene that finds its protagonist, the 'seedy solipsist', seeking gainful employment as a 'smart boy' at a chandlery in Gray's Inn Road only to be met with ridicule:

> ' 'E ain't smart,' said the chandler, 'not by a long chork 'e ain't.'
> 'Nor 'e ain't a boy,' said the chandler's semi-private convenience, 'not to my mind 'e ain't.' ' 'E don't look rightly human to me,' said the chandlers' eldest waste product, 'not rightly.' (Beckett, 2009a, 50)

All too familiar with this kind of abuse, Murphy wanders off and looks for somewhere to rest his weary mind and body: 'There was nowhere. There had once been a small public garden south of the Royal Free Hospital, but now part of it lay buried under one of those malignant proliferations of urban tissue known as service flats and the rest was reserved for the bacteria' (50). The processes of urban development have made London an inhospitable site for Beckett's protagonist, who finds himself cast out from municipal spaces by these private developments, which offer their inhabitants housekeeping, prepared meals and other services. When he tries to identify another possible public space where he can gather himself, Murphy can only think of Lincoln's Inn Fields: 'The atmosphere there was foul, a miasma of laws. Those of the cozeners, crossbiting and conycatching and sacking and figging; and those of the cozened, pillory, and gallows. But there was grass and there were plane trees' (51). Any possibility of finding a hospitable site of leisure again founders, this time owing to a web of regulations meant, in former times, to protect potential victims from various crimes and deceptions, but which now inflict themselves on the freedom of the city dweller.

Beckett's protagonist does, at times, resist these commercial and bureaucratic forces with a variety of little stratagems and, in doing so, calls attention to other possibilities for everyday life in this context. For instance, in addition to his persistent habit of rocking himself into a catatonic stupor, Murphy can also be found strolling the streets of the city in a series of repetitive, nearly obsessive perambulations that defy the planned and programmed character of urban space. I have written at some length elsewhere (Bixby, 2009, 102–5) about how his elaborate itineraries evoke what Michel de Certeau, in *The Practice of Everyday Life* (1984), describes as a 'rhetoric of walking' that enables 'users' to appropriate an urban system organised by various structures of authority. For de Certeau, the urban narrative composed by pedestrians transforms the rationalised organisation of space, as the 'planned and readable city' yields to a '*migrational*, or metaphorical, city' constituted by their 'turns of phrase' or the 'stylistic figures' (de Certeau, 1984, 93, 100; emphasis in original). We might connect this with what Lefebvre calls the 'reappropriation' of space by ordinary city dwellers, who play a role in shaping the urban environment to conform to their own needs and desires (Lefebvre, 1991, 56). This is not to suggest that Murphy should be taken for a flaneur who enjoys the indulgences tendered by the accumulated capital of the metropolis and delights in the spectacle of the city, including its colourful working-class inhabitants. Instead, Beckett's down-and-out protagonist might be conceived as a satirical response to the privileged position of the metropolitan flaneur and his unimpeded mobility.

His compulsive walking is just one of several practices that Murphy seems to have developed precisely to opt out of metropolitan capitalism, to avoid being swept into its vast machinery and the routinised lives of its labourers. When compelled to look for employment, he devises a long route – from Kings Cross up Caledonian Road and eventually past Market Road Gardens and around Pentonville Prison – to occupy his afternoon, rather than spend the entire day on the job hunt. Although he lives in penury, Murphy manages to avoid work for a time through an advantageous arrangement with his uncle, who provides a monthly allowance for his rent, and his landlady, who skims off a small amount and returns it to her tenant: 'This superb arrangement enabled him to consume away at pretty well his own gait, but was inadequate for a domestic establishment, no matter how frugal' (Beckett, 2009a, 14). As the novel tracks his movements around London, it notes the modest expenditures that keep body and soul together – 'the fourpence he allowed himself to be allowed for his lunch' and so forth (53). It also describes the small stratagems that enable Murphy to 'swindle' a restaurant 'every day of his lunch, to the honourable extent of paying for one cup of tea and consuming 1.83 cups', a scheme undertaken with 'satisfaction, because the supreme moment in his degradations had come, the moment when, unaided and alone, he defrauded a vested interest' (53). Although the amount involved is small, it nonetheless signifies a meaningful achievement: 'no matter how the transactions were judged from the economic point of view, nothing could detract from its merit as a little triumph of tactics in the face of the most fearful odds' (53). Rather than retreating into private consciousness, Murphy applies his mind to concrete matters, offering Beckett an occasion to critique the alienating social and economic conditions of metropolitan capitalism.

This critique takes on a new dimension when Murphy finally takes up employment at the Magdalen Mental Mercyseat or 'M.M.M.', 'a hospital for the better-class mentally deranged' on the outskirts of the city (Beckett, 2009a, 56). With this new setting, the novel offers a counterpoint to the enduring anxiety, alienation and dissatisfaction of everyday life in the nominally free society of the British capital, even as it explores forms of alienation that belong to these new circumstances as well. Psychiatric hospitals are what Foucault calls 'heterotopias of deviation: those in which individuals are put whose behaviour is deviant with respect to the mean or the required norm' (Foucault, 1986, 24).[8] Separated from the general

---

[8] I first described Beckett's representation of the M.M.M. as a 'heterotopia of deviation' in *Samuel Beckett and the Postcolonial Novel* (Bixby, 2009, 111–16). Subsequently, James Little has developed this idea in relation to this and other institutional spaces in *Samuel Beckett in Confinement: The Politics of Closed Space* (2020, 25–32, 82–7).

population, disengaged from the demands of the outside world, these spaces create a boundary between what modern societies consider 'normal' and 'deviant' human behaviour. The M.M.M., however, offers Murphy a site where he can practise his eccentric meditations without the interruptions of social and economic necessity that afflict him in London. In this sense, he adopts the asylum as a refuge from the realm of everyday life, even if he must perform a series of daily duties: 'to make beds, carry trays, clean up regular messes, clean up casual messes, read thermometers, write charts, wash the bedridden, give medicine, hose down its effects, warm bedpans, cool fevers, boil gags, sterilize when in doubt' (95). In this sense, then, the tasks repeated day after day, without variation or novelty, persist in the M.M.M., but they have been severed from the common settings that Lefebvre associates with the quotidian – in short, they present an image of the everyday made strange.

Inhabiting their heterotopia of deviation, the inmates of the M.M.M. may be seen as exemplars of pathological withdrawal at odds with the arbiters of social reality: Murphy identifies in the various melancholics, paranoids, hebephrenics, hymonics and schizoids 'a race of people he had long since despaired of finding', located in a liminal space that mocks the strivings of 'reasonable' men in the outside world (Beckett, 2009a, 106). The M.M.M. thus prompts a questioning of what is considered 'normal' or 'natural', in both literary representation and human behaviour, opening up possibilities for other ways of thinking and living. The asylum, in short, generates a sense of defamiliarisation and a form of detachment from the domain of everyday life. In this way, Beckett's novel engages in the critique of everyday life as Lefebvre's philosophy outlines it, refusing to accept the quotidian passively, to apprehend it *qua* quotidian, and instead helping us view it from an alternative perspective. There is a significant irony lurking here insofar as Murphy's idealisation of the M.M.M. overlooks both the profound weariness of the inmates and the disciplinary function of the asylum. If he venerates the patients for their general rejection of the everyday world, the doctors nonetheless treat them with the aim of re-establishing their contact with social reality. Murphy may have left behind the familiar settings of the capitalist metropolis, but he has not managed to escape, not entirely, the pervasive socio-economic forces that were imposed on him in those settings. To be sure, the pervasiveness of those alienating influences is highlighted by their persistence even in the space of the M.M.M.

Mr Knott's estate, the setting of much of Beckett's next novel, *Watt* (1953), functions as a heterotopian space much like the M.M.M., where the various norms established in the outside world are simultaneously represented, contested and overturned. The narrative begins in something like the familiar world of the realist novel, depicting the lives of ordinary people in everyday circumstances and focusing on their character traits, social relations and physical surroundings in a place resembling Dublin. But the narrative soon moves, with its eponymous protagonist, out beyond the city to the disconcerting world of the estate, where Watt immediately encounters strange circumstances that will confound his attempts at explanation for as long as he resides there.

The estate is a setting for the mundane activities of everyday life, of its routines, repetitions and rhythms, of Watt's quotidian labours as a domestic servant; yet, as he soon learns from his predecessor in the role, Arsene, the estate is also a place that unsettles these daily routines. Arsene tells Watt of the day when he first sensed this disturbing shift, which he insists was not simply internal or subjective and implies is the reason for his impending departure:

> Something slipped. There I was, warm and bright, smoking my tobacco-pipe, watching the warm bright wall, when suddenly somewhere some little thing slipped, some little tiny thing. [...] It was a slip like that I felt, that Tuesday afternoon, millions of little things moving all together out of their old place, into a new one nearby, and furtively, as though it were forbidden. (Beckett, 2009b, 34)

If Arsene's admission is one of the first clues that there is something strange about this place, the flood of words that follows, providing a detailed account of his time on the estate and much that came before, demonstrates that it will not be easily comprehended. Is the estate a site of epistemological disruption? Of labour exploitation? Of divine mystery? Of class oppression? Of absolute unreason? Perhaps, as Lefebvre suggests of Kafka's *The Castle* and the fate of its protagonist K (who is also summoned by an enigmatic authority to perform a job), the essential thing in Beckett's novel is that the everyday life of modern man is 'tragically controlled by unresolved contradictions and by the most painful contradiction of all: that between absurdity and Reason, both equally inhuman, both indivisibly united' (Lefebvre, 2002, 264). The crucial difference between *The Castle* and *Watt*, however, is that the latter treats this contradiction not just at the level of content but at that of form, which manifests the absurdity that arises precisely from the pursuit of rational explanations.

Set off from the rest of the world, Mr Knott's estate gives place to puzzling phenomena that both demand and defy Watt's attempts at interpretation. Critics have often cited these phenomena to advance the claim that the novel is concerned with the inadequacies of language or the failure of words and things to coincide (along with the implications of these failures for literary realism), while giving little attention to what they might mean for the representation of everyday life in the novel. But *Watt*, like *Murphy*, is a novel very much concerned with the function of dreary routines. It soon becomes clear that, although Watt never has any 'direct dealings' with Mr Knott, his daily rhythms are dictated by the eccentric demands of his master, whose own habits vary greatly:

> one of the first things that Watt learned [...] was that Mr Knott sometimes rose late and retired early, and sometimes rose very late and retired very early, and sometimes did not rise at all, nor at all retire, for who can retire who does not rise. (Beckett, 2009b, 68)

The directives handed down by Mr Knott are usually detailed, often in the extreme, but they do not seem to follow any principle of efficiency, and their rationale remains mysterious to Watt and his co-workers. Each morning, for instance, slops must be brought down to the ground floor to be emptied, but 'not in the way that slops are usually emptied, no, but in the garden, before sunrise, or after sunset, on the violet bed in the violet time, and on the pansy bed in the pansy time', and so on (53). Later, we learn of the detailed weekly preparations of Mr Knott's meals, a peculiar concoction served to the master, 'cold, in a bowl, at twelve o'clock noon sharp and at seven p.m. exactly, all the year round', although Watt never sees his master at mealtime because Mr Knott arrives in the dining room at irregular times, as they suit him (70). Further, we learn that 'Watt's instructions were to give what Mr Knott left of this dish, on days when he did not eat it all, to the dog', although there is no dog living on the grounds of the estate (72). The servant's desire – one might say, mania – to follow the instructions of his master to the letter, no matter how absurd, leads Watt through a series of reflections on how to secure a hungry dog at the right time that go on for nearly ten pages.

The result of these often-perplexing instructions is the creation of working conditions characterised by confusion, isolation and disempowerment, which leave Watt overwhelmed and incapable of deriving meaningful experience from his occupation. Again, but now more radically, more thoroughly, Beckett's novel demonstrates that, despite the impulses of his protagonist, there is no possibility of the subject somehow escaping intact from social and economic imperatives, which penetrate the deepest recesses of everyday life. Concealed beneath the superficial rationality of the Knott estate's management lies deeper irrationality, but below this lurks an even deeper dehumanised and dehumanising rationality. The estate comes to epitomise a site of mystified capitalist exploitation, something akin to a private plantation, industrial factory, or company town. That the demands on Watt are rendered so hyperbolically only heightens this image of alienation, which reduces him to a mere function of his social and economic circumstances. That he struggles so mightily to make sense of his experience, and yet fails to comprehend the mechanisms at work, suggests the disorienting and damaging effects of these surroundings.

The story of Watt's stay at Mr Knott's house repeatedly demonstrates his difficulties in transcribing even the most mundane events into terms that promise any satisfactory coherence or transparency. But, in precisely this way, the novel begins to render visible the elusive qualities of the everyday. It is not long until Watt encounters something like the slippage described by Arsene, an experience brought on by the arrival of the Galls, a father and son duo, who come to the estate to tune the piano. This seemingly banal occasion becomes an object of obsessive contemplation, replaying itself over and over in his mind, as Watt attempts to make sense of this quotidian 'incident'. 'Followed by others of a similar kind, incidents that is to say of great formal brilliance and indeterminable purport', the incident establishes a pattern that will characterise his entire stay at the estate: 'Watt [finds] himself in the midst of things which, if they consented to be named, did so as it were with reluctance' (Beckett, 2009b, 59, 64). He experiences a linguistic slippage that disrupts even his most routine efforts to attach names to things, as in the oft-cited 'pot' passage:

> And the state in which Watt found himself resisted formulation in a way no state had ever done, in which Watt had ever found himself, and Watt had found himself in a great many states, in his day. Looking at a pot, for example, or thinking of a pot, at one of Mr Knott's pots, of one of Mr Knott's pots, it was in vain that Watt said, Pot, pot. Well perhaps not quite in vain, but very nearly. For it was not a pot, the more he looked, the more he reflected, the more he felt sure of that, that it was not a pot at all. It resembled a pot, it was almost a pot, but it was not a pot of which one could say, Pot, pot, and be comforted. (64)

Here, the novel suggests that the ways in which both scientific empiricism and literary realism encourage us to pay attention to the world of ordinary things utterly fail, so that Watt's experience of the object and his inability to capture it in words work to disturb any comfortable sense of the everyday. In these circumstances, moreover, everyday language – with its comfortable and clichéd modes of expression – gives way to Watt's frantic linguistic efforts to capture what suddenly seems incomprehensible.

The pot is an utterly banal object, but its banality is precisely what is most crucial here because it nonetheless escapes every linguistic formulation, all consistency or regularity. In this sense, it becomes a telling metonym for the everyday because it appears to belong to insignificance and yet it also seems to demand signification – and, in doing so, shows us how the everyday often eludes the regimes of representation altogether. The passage dedicated to it forms a late modernist response to the art of everyday life, which does not rescue, 'one after the other, each facet of the quotidian from anonymity' like *Ulysses* but rather accentuates the ways that the everyday escapes linguistic expression and rational inquiry. *Watt*, then, is not only a text concerned with abstract inquiries into scientific empiricism or literary realism but one also concerned with probing both the pervasive slipperiness of everyday life and the alienating forces at work in its deepest recesses. Moreover, the novel represents a turning point in Beckett's career not just because it portrays a mind confronting the limits of language or the boundaries of human knowledge but because it pursues these inquiries in relation to a heterotopian space that allows us to see more clearly the linguistic and epistemological conundrums attending all efforts to come to terms with quotidian experience.

To describe the shift in Beckett's writing in this way is to defend its increasing abstraction against accusations that it leads directly to resignation, meaninglessness, or even nihilism. In 'The Ideology of Modernism', after dismissing Beckett's writing as symptomatic of pathological withdrawal, Lukács also claims that Kafka's fiction 'has emptied everyday life of meaning by using the allegorical method; he has allowed detail to be annihilated by his transcendental nothingness' and this 'prevents him from investing observed detail with typical significance'. Therefore, his writing cannot 'achieve that fusion of the particular and the general which is the essence of realist art' since it instead pushes individuation in the direction of abstraction and abnegates all responsibility to social or historical matters (Lukács, 1963, 45). For Lukács, in short, modernism renders the individual isolated and the world unintelligible. In *The Critique of Everyday Life, Volume 1*, Lefebvre alludes to a similar accusation levelled by 'the Marxist dialectician [...] at modern French literature as a whole': 'that it expresses individuality, but rather that it expresses only false individuality, a façade of individuality, and abstraction' (Lefebvre, 2002, 257). Although Lefebvre does not absolve Beckett's writing from this sin, he does claim a few pages later that Kafka's work should not be condemned for forsaking quotidian experience: his '"universe" is not and is not intended to be extraordinary, nor does it aspire to be a universe; it is everyday life – Kafka's view of it – meticulously described and captured in its essence' (264).

Much the same could be said of Mr Knott's estate in *Watt* and Beckett's approach to everyday life in his mid-career fiction. But where Lefebvre's emphasis falls on the force of descriptive detail in Kafka's work, which aligns with his own interest in intricate modes of sociological analysis, Beckett's work pushes all efforts at describing the everyday to the point of semiotic instability and even linguistic failure – though, as I have argued, this is a significant failure. In his radical formal experimentation, Beckett presents everyday life on the estate with both specificity and an aura of abstraction, so that what is seemingly given or substantial becomes elusive. In this regard, we encounter something like a negative image of the quotidian. Watt's obsessive inquiries into the phenomena of Mr Knott's estate, which generate all manner of repetitions, inversions and other permutations (and which, as we learn, are filtered through the perspective of another narrator), force a critical detachment on the reader, who encounters the quotidian in a radically enigmatic and *nearly* unintelligible form that, despite all this, retains a relation with the most ordinary and mundane features of everyday life. Beckett's novel thus provides a potential site for the critique of everyday life in capitalist society, which stands outside the epistemological assumptions of both literary realism and high modernism. In doing so, moreover, *Watt* disrupts the reigning illusions that suggest that everyday life possesses a substantial reality that cannot possibly be any different.

2 Almost a Routine, Twice: *Waiting for Godot* and *Endgame*

If the most familiar axiom in Beckett criticism is that his writing moves progressively towards abstraction, minimalism and even nullity during his long career, this truism generally fails to account for how his work continues nonetheless to speak to the mundane details of everyday life in the modern world. It is worth noting that this movement towards abstraction began in earnest during Beckett's wartime experience and especially during his period in Roussillon, where he composed the majority of *Watt* in the anxious (though often tedious and even mundane) circumstances of his work with the Resistance. The famous doodles in the *Watt* manuscript, as odd and ornate as they are, speak to the tedium of the writing process and the need to kill time during long periods of waiting between night-time intelligence operations. After the dangers of the initial invasion, the conditions of the German occupation were such that the everyday was restored to some kind of regular rhythm, albeit one characterised by new deprivations. If everyday life was more fragile and perilous in these conditions, the daily routines of working, eating and waiting still formed an oddly familiar, if remarkably diminished, sense of the quotidian.

Liberation, as Lefebvre would emphasise, quickly brought a new optimism and a sense that life would soon be utterly transformed, which contributed to the remarkably rapid modernisation of France after the war, including a rush towards American-style consumerism. Years of conflict had torn down the old structures of French society and suggested the possibility of rebuilding things from the ground up, even if those hopes were largely disappointed by the realities of post-war France. It was in this context that Lefebvre published the first volume of his massive *Critique of Everyday Life* (1947); it was also in this context that Beckett began to write his iconic *Waiting for Godot* (1952).[9] Beckett's theatrical experiments through the next decade and beyond can be seen as so many efforts to address, however obliquely, the changing coordinates of the everyday in these new cultural, political and economic circumstances. Rather than critiquing everyday life in the name of Truth or Being or some more profound reality, Beckett's drama approaches the banality and terror of everyday life from the inside, with attention to routine activities, mundane objects and bodily contingencies. In the process, his plays reveal something extraordinary in the ordinary, not by presenting it as a content or theme so much as by generating a negativity that throws the matters of everyday life into a sharper relief and allows his audience to reconsider their potentiality.

In a sense, *Waiting for Godot* is self-evidently about the everyday. This play, in which 'nothing happens, twice', is largely made up of inconspicuous behaviours, a series of habitual actions and verbal gestures that carry the two protagonists, Vladimir and Estragon, through the course of a day (or Act One). And then, just to be sure we understand the repetitiveness of their lives, the play presents another day (or Act Two), during which the protagonists carry on much as they had before. If nothing else, the play impresses upon us the knowledge that the transit through today has been much like the transit through yesterday and will be much like the transit through tomorrow: 'One knows what to expect', as Estragon remarks (Beckett, 1986, 37). In the process, the play demonstrates for us the various ways that the protagonists get through their days, accompanied by the petty irritations and minor dissatisfactions that punctuate their boredom or depression. The scarcity of action, of development, of denouement suggests something about how the everyday slips outside the structures of narrative temporality and maintains a certain disordered, amorphous quality. If the play evokes certain allegorical parallels, it nonetheless eludes correspondences with both divine and human myths. In the summer of 1953, writing to Carlheinz Caspari ahead of the German premiere of *Waiting for Godot*, Beckett denied that the play had any symbolist or expressionist elements and instead stressed that 'first and foremost, it is a question of something that happens, almost a routine, and it is this dailiness and this materiality, in my view, that need to be brought out' (Beckett, 2011, 391). Indeed, tragicomedy might be the most apt genre for addressing the everyday insofar as it suggests a heightened awareness and intensity that promises a glimpse of something beyond the limitations of everyday life, coupled with the mundane concerns and repetitive tasks that contribute to a sense of emptiness and alienation in

---

[9] Find these works in Lefebvre (2002) and Beckett (1986).

quotidian experience. Lefebvre claims that repetition has come to dominate everyday life in no small part because it tends to suppress the fear of death: 'It dissimulates the tragic' (Lefebvre, 1988, 80). Vladimir and Estragon may be impatiently anticipating some kind of final outcome, but they persist precisely through a series of daily routines that help to distract them from their purpose.

These features of *Waiting for Godot* have often led critics to attribute Existentialist ideas to the play, insofar as their perpetual waiting seems to defy any clear purpose or final resolution and instead gestures towards the absurdity of the human desire for meaning in a meaningless universe. The drawn-out frustrations of Vladimir and Estragon thus suggest some generalisable human condition characterised by physical and emotional suffering without inherent significance. Their experience of everyday life seems to be defined precisely by this burden. The most that can be said about the pair is that they have attempted to impose some kind of meaning on the everyday precisely in the act of waiting, whether or not their endurance will ever be rewarded: 'Yes,' Vladimir reflects, 'in this immense confusion one thing alone is clear. We are waiting for Godot to come—' (Beckett, 1986, 74).

Readings of the play's presumed absurdity have often relied on its apparent placelessness – '*A country road. A tree. Evening.*' – to confirm its philosophical significance (Beckett, 1986, 11). To be sure, the setting suggests a utopia in the literal meaning of that term, a 'no place', desolate and isolated, where no specific position in a historical period or a geographical locale can be established. This negation and abstraction, in turn, has been construed as a retreat from history to a domain where nothing remains except the barest residue of social reality (and perhaps not even so much as that). In addition to suggesting the play's absurdity, this seeming 'worldlessness' has authorised a range of allegorical interpretations identifying *Waiting for Godot* as a response to a domain devastated by war or simply to the alienating conditions of modernity, which has abandoned the sustaining myths of previous eras. However, if we view the evacuated stage as a heterotopia, standing in critical relation to social reality, then we can better see how the play exposes the everyday to negativity in historically significant ways – precisely by breaking the spell of social reality, of 'worldliness' and its hold over our actions and reactions. Adorno reads such abstraction in Beckett's writing as 'an objectively motivated loss of the object', so that 'this shabby, damaged world of images is the negative imprint of the administered world' (Adorno, 1997, 31). In this way, we might add, his writing helps us to perceive the aftermath of the war and the emergence of late capitalism in attenuated images of everyday life, positioned within a vision of near total political, cultural and social collapse, and it encourages us to re-examine the practices, behaviours and social norms that make up quotidian existence under these historical conditions.

Crucially, the nearly bare stage is not entirely nowhere, not simply a bland nothingness or existential void or timeless space of being as such. By virtue of a series of telling hints in the dialogue, critics and theatre practitioners have considered the space not just in relation to the recent war but in relation to Irish history and other circumstances of poverty, deprivation and weariness. We are invited, if we are attuned to both the implications of these fleeting allusions and the critique of everyday life, to imagine the actions and utterances on stage with respect to these circumstances and to consider the damage they have inflicted on individuals and communities. And yet, as Adorno noted, 'even where reality finds entry into the narrative, precisely at those points at which reality threatens to suppress what the literary subject once performed, it is evident that there is something uncanny about this reality' (Adorno, 1997, 31). The fleeting markers of a reality beyond the stage or page do not provide us with a firm grounding in a specific social setting or collection of historical circumstances but instead render everyday life strange and enigmatic. If Lefebvre identifies a similar capacity in examples of the 'new novel' in post-war France – which, according to his reading, offer no acknowledged, pre-established referents, only unnamed places of desolation and destruction – then here we can take up their 'further ramifications' for Beckett's drama and 'contemporary theatre' that his analysis declines to pursue (Lefebvre, 1971, 11). Beckett's formal innovations suggest an alternative, however bleak, to the totalising embrace of everyday life in the modern world, but this is not merely a retreat from the world into abstraction. His austere scenarios generate a negativity that presents the everyday (all that is empirical, concrete, practical) in a radically different light and holds open a space, however narrow, for a world we cannot yet imagine.

Beckett's evacuated settings nonetheless accommodate a number of objects that tether the action of the plays to the everyday world (even as they are reminders that Beckett's theatre still adheres to the theatrical conventions of props and costuming, with their reminders of empirical social reality, no matter how abstract or non-referential his plays may appear to be). When the curtain rises on Act One, we find Estragon seated on the mound at centre stage as he struggles and eventually fails to remove one of his worn-out boots. Immediately, then, we are drawn to the daily ritual of putting on and taking off footwear, that familiar, humble and mundane item, along with the intransigence of such objects even to our most basic desires; we are introduced to a sense of the dreary, perfunctory and repetitive quality of the everyday, which places individuals in a position barely distinguishable from the world of objects they inhabit; we are faced with a Chaplinesque reminder that even in the unfamiliar world on the stage we encounter familiar objects and we laugh in recognition at our own battles with trivial things. At the outset, the play also tells us that this fate is to be expected for a down-and-out tramp, who does not have the wherewithal to acquire his own pair of well-fitting shoes. Estragon's opening words, 'nothing to be done', so often taken in the broadest and most abstract sense, as existential resignation at the absurdity of human endeavour, is more immediately, more directly, a comment on his struggle with everyday objects (Beckett, 1986, 11). Although the evacuated setting, which ostensibly removes such items from their social and economic contexts, begs us to import a broader meaning, Estragon's most pressing concern is simply his inability to make the material world conform to his desires. Indeed, Vladimir's response – 'I'm beginning to come around to that opinion' – seems to encourage some larger, more abstract significance, even if this may be indicative only of his own 'abstraction', his insensitivity to the actual troubles of his colleague (and even if this reflection is firmly tethered to the objective circumstances of the pair) (11). In any case, Estragon's material 'struggle' with the shoes and Vladimir's existential 'struggle', his lifelong battle for happiness or fulfilment or meaning, are closely linked in the opening lines of the play.

Despite its flirtations with abstraction and its various invitations to metaphysical interpretation, the play persistently focuses attention on mundane objects that connect its action and dialogue to material concerns. While Estragon repeatedly struggles with his boot during the course of the play, Vladimir offers him a series of root vegetables – a carrot, a turnip, a radish – as the two perform their daily routines. The property list for *Godot* includes not just root vegetables but rubbish, spectacles, bowler hats, a watch, a pipe, a box of matches, a handkerchief and other everyday objects that generate a tenuous 'reality effect' and associate the strange world of the play with something more recognisable. In doing so, of course, they also provide some suggestions regarding the economic circumstances and class positioning of the characters: yes, Vladimir and Estragon appear to be vagabonds who find themselves without a home, destitute and rather down at heel, beyond the limits of bourgeois respectability and the embrace of bourgeois society; yes, Pozzo, with his spectacles, watch, pipe and so forth (not to mention his manservant), appears to be a man of means or at least one who aspires to an aristocratic image. Recently, William Davies and James McNaughton have both argued – in books exploring the impact of the Second World War on Beckett's literary imagination – that the meagre supplies possessed by Vladimir and Estragon also suggest the conditions the author experienced first-hand in Paris and Roussillon. Of course, if the play is in some sense 'about' the war and its aftermath, it addresses the base matters of food, rationing and unemployment, rather than the political dramas acted out at the level of prime ministers, parliamentary debates and national policies. Davies stresses the importance of hunger as a fact of everyday life during the conflict, so that the dwindling foodstuffs in the play suggest the harsh realities of the German occupation and the daily struggle to survive that became 'its unremarkable remarkability' as the conflict dragged on (Davies, 2020, 73). McNaughton develops this theme through an extended reading of the later *Endgame* in relation to the famine politics of the 1930s and 1940s, which convincingly challenges Leo Bersani and Ulysse Duthoit's influential Existentialist interpretation of the play as a meditation on 'time-as-death' (Bersani and Dutoit, 1993, 41), by highlighting the historical concerns of food power and grain hoarding that pervade the entire drama (McNaughton, 2018, 137–63).

Hunger, deprivation and declining health became quotidian in these circumstances, which highlight the desire for physical comfort as much as any grand metaphysical questions or stirring humanistic responses to universal suffering. The visual irony generated by Estragon's line 'I'll go and get a carrot', accompanied by the stage direction '*he does not move*', becomes something other than absurd – it becomes a poignant reminder of material deprivations (Beckett, 1986, 64). The tramp, as Lefebvre suggests of Chaplin, presents a 'pure negative image' in the complete alienation of the human and the embodied critique of nominally free society. But where Chaplin presents a 'myth' that is 'directly accessible to the masses' and 'uses laughter to stir the masses profoundly', Beckett refuses to create a new mythology around his tramps (Lefebvre, 2002, 34–5). He does not insert his tramps in settings that can be readily identified as the city, the factory, the war, fascism and so on. His art nonetheless presents us with what Lefebvre calls the 'complex problem' of the negative image insofar as he deploys figures that appear to be in some sense deviant and settings that seem quite different from the everyday, precisely to critique social reality (34).

Of course, what sustains a reading of *Waiting for Godot* as a critical engagement, however oblique and attenuated, with everyday life is the prominence of routine and habit in the action of the play. Beginning with Martin Esslin, critics have often extrapolated from Beckett's reading of Proust's novels to interpretations of the play, arguing that 'the routine of waiting for Godot stands for habit, which prevents us from reaching the painful, but fruitful, awareness of the full reality of being' (Esslin, 1961, 59). In this sense, habit and routine provide an escape, however fleeting, from the anxiety of the uncertain and unknown, especially the great unknown of death: if 'the air is full of our cries', as Vladimir reflects, in a moment of sudden clarity, then 'habit is a great deadener' (Beckett, 1986, 84). It may be true that everyday repetition 'dissimulates the tragic', but Lefebvre also reminds us that repetition is the modality of administered society and the basis for exploitation and domination. Even in highly developed late capitalist societies, very few groups free themselves from the regular schedule of deep-seated customs linked with cyclic time, including eating, resting and sleeping. The performance of these behaviours against the evacuated backdrop of the play *re*-presents them, gives them the impression of something a bit strange, uncanny, and thus exemplifies the functioning of habit and routine with different inflections, especially amid such deprivation and destitution. What is one to do when there is no work to be done? Vladimir and Estragon do manage to get through the day and then the next: 'I tell you I wasn't doing anything', pleads Estragon; 'Perhaps you weren't. But it's the way of doing it that counts, the way of doing it, if you want to go on living', replies Vladimir (55). Forsaken in this isolated wasteland, experiencing nothing but quotidian repetition and unending routine, Beckett's tramps confront what Blanchot calls 'the dangerous essence of the everyday', which seizes them with an uneasiness each time they step back and face its apparent nullity (Blanchot, 1987, 19).

The routinisation of everyday life for Vladimir and Estragon is perhaps most evident in their speech, which is highlighted by the reduced circumstances in which they converse. With some self-awareness about the routine character of their activity, they reflect that conversation might just help pass the time as they wait and that it might even alleviate their anxieties about waiting in the process. In these strange circumstances, their dialogue takes on a particular quality closely related to Blanchot's descriptions of everyday speech:

> What is proper to the everyday is that it designates for us a region, or a level of speech, where the determinations true and false, like the opposition yes and no, do not apply—it being always before what affirms it and yet incessantly reconstituting itself beyond all that negates it. An unserious seriousness from which nothing can divert us, even when it is lived in the mode of diversion; so we experience it through the boredom that seems to be indeed the sudden, the insensible apprehension of the quotidian into which one slides in the leveling of a steady slack time, feeling oneself forever sucked in, though feeling at the same time that one has already lost it, and is henceforth incapable of deciding if there is a lack of the everyday, or if one has too much of it. (Blanchot, 1987, 16)

More than anything, Vladimir and Estragon's speech trades in banalities, commonplaces and redundancies, which might lead them to the threshold of some insight, only to stumble, cease and begin again with more banalities. Often their speech amounts to not much more than phatic communication, which does not convey any information but rather serves a simple social function such as establishing or maintaining contact and creating a general sense of sociality between interlocutors. Their discourse also shares this much with what Heidegger calls 'idle talk', which is mainly concerned with carrying out the exchange smoothly and effectively, rather than with providing any genuine understanding of the topic at hand or the world in general. This suggests the possibility of reading the play as a Heideggerian allegory in which idle speech alternately distracts and fails to distract us from the brute reality of existence. But, for Blanchot, this region of speech is of interest not because it masks some deeper reality or distracts from authentic being but rather because it provides a mode of persistence in the face of boredom that nonetheless affords little purchase on quotidian experience.

Beckett emphasises the function of such speech at several points during the play, just when the two tramps seem to be on the cusp of some insight amid their repetitive daily rounds. But, on the nearly bare stage, largely detached from historical referents, what Beckett offers is less a reiteration of 'everyday speech' than a metalanguage addressed to 'everyday speech', so that the words of his characters become a means to reflect on this region of discourse. When, in the opening pages of the play, Vladimir broaches the subject of the fate of the two thieves crucified alongside Christ, he repeats the perspectives offered by the four Evangelists, but he does so merely to initiate an exchange: 'Come on, Estragon, return the ball, can't you, once in a way' (Beckett, 1986, 14). Vladimir carries on in the hope of arriving at some kind of ethical or scriptural insight that might overcome the consensus, based on just one of the Evangelists, that one of the thieves was saved. 'Who believes him?', asks Estragon. 'Everybody. It's the only version they know', replies Vladimir, to which Estragon can only respond, 'People are bloody ignorant apes' (15). But that is as far as they can take their inquiry before it dies out, Vladimir having repeated everything he has heard about the subject, it seems. The exchange introduces ideas about faith and salvation into *Waiting for Godot*, playfully inviting theological or metaphysical interpretations, but Beckett also holds up such exchanges for our inspection, as if calling us to see them for what they clearly are – mundane and confused. Later, when Vladimir launches into his famous soliloquy, he presents us again with the possibility of some penetrating insight that promises to transcend the limitations of everyday speech: 'Was I sleeping, while the others suffered? Am I sleeping now? Tomorrow, when I wake, or think I do, what shall I say of today?' (84). He takes the language he has at his disposal and, through a series of self-directed questions, attempts to guide his thoughts towards some correct or reliable understanding of the world. But, without an interlocutor, his efforts quickly dissipate and come to exemplify the self-foundering character of speech in the face of the quotidian.

The language of *Endgame* shares much with the language of *Waiting for Godot*, although it is uttered in the circumstances not of anticipation but of aftermath.

Certainly, the plays also share in their spare stage dressing – '*Bare interior. Grey light.*' – and yet the later drama presses the negation of social and cultural details to what might seem an apocalyptic extreme, whether this negation is owed to world war, nuclear annihilation, climate catastrophe, or some other cause (Beckett, 1986, 92). *Endgame* thus confronts everyday life with images from some other place, some other time. In their 'shelter', with its two small windows, two ashbins covered with an old sheet (and occupied by the unseen Nagg and Nell) and one picture with its face to the wall, Hamm and Clov occupy a space that seems almost too spare, too forlorn, to be any kind of proper home, though it nevertheless gives place to their daily routines. When Clov peers out of the windows, he reports only the bleakest of conditions: '[*He looks, moving the telescope*] Zero ... [*he looks*] ... zero [*he looks*] ... and zero. ... Corpsed' (106). In this atmosphere of perpetual aftermath, where 'there's no more nature', it appears as if the quotidian activities of the world outside have finally ceased, even though the signs of everyday life in the shelter display a certain continuity with what came before this rupture. As Stanley Cavell claimed in his influential early essay on the play, 'to miss the ordinariness of the lives in *Endgame* is to avoid the extraordinariness (and ordinariness) of our own' (Cavell, 1976, 150). With not much else to occupy themselves in their radically diminished circumstances, Hamm and Clov rely on a few well-worn daily rituals and their rather strained verbal repartee, which seems to do little more than bore them: they discuss the weather, ask each other how they feel, trade a variety of insults, make a few impotent threats and tell stories that they have surely heard many times before. For Cavell, the language of Hamm and Clov sometimes sounds 'extraordinary', but it generally mimics 'the qualities of ordinary conversation among people whose world is shared – catching its abrupt shifts and sudden continuities; its shades of memory, regret, intimidation; its opacity to the outsider' (150). The play provides us with one example after another of something like everyday speech, drawing attention to a level of discourse where subject matter and truth value are secondary to simply maintaining verbal intercourse:

Hamm: We're not beginning to ... to ... mean something?
Clov: Mean something! You and I, mean something! (*Brief laugh*.) Ah that's a good one!'(Beckett, 1986, 108)

Adorno takes this analysis a step further to suggest that 'gaps open up between the mechanically assembled phrases of everyday speech', so that such instances of 'linguistic shrugging of the shoulders' become 'apocalyptic precisely by virtue of [their] utter familiarity'. Everyday speech, with its accumulated cliches, hackneyed phrases and assumption of common sense, begins to confess its own meaninglessness, even 'its own nihilism' (Adorno, 1991, 256).

Much of the dialogue, we might add, is routine or even *a* routine, *a theatrical* routine, as has often been noted. But because these are routines played out in an environment seemingly stripped of the social and institutional accoutrements of everyday life, from community to bureaucracy and government, the dialogue begins to take on startling new dimensions. To be sure, the evacuated setting again produces a heightened theatricality at times, especially in those metalinguistic and metatheatrical moments when Hamm, the ham actor and theatrical descendant of Hamlet, draws on the theatrical tradition for his speech: 'Let us not waste our time in idle discourse' (Beckett, 1986, 74). It is as if, in baring the stage and raising the curtain on this dysfunctional family, Beckett is showing us both the derivative nature of everyday speech and the performative quality of everyday life in a dark mirror, where the characters become actors playing their roles. In other words, the stage does not provide us with a representation of the real, some moment in human history, or some context of historical events, although it does offer us a version of social reality in the theatre. Adorno suggests that 'Beckett stares at such things until the everyday family life from which they are drawn pales into irrelevance', and they are 'structured into a second, autonomous context' as they are 'emancipated from their context and from the character's personality' (Adorno, 1991, 249). We might call this a second-order realism, according to which the verisimilitude of the play should be sought not in its referential function but, rather, in the extension of its metalinguistic and metatheatrical functions: 'the absurdity of talk does not unfold in opposition to realism but rather develops out of it' (256). Hamm plays at the familiar roles of domineering patriarch, master of the house and so on, delivering his lines as if they were scripted by social codes that have otherwise been wiped away from a ruined planet.

At times, the characters seem to perceive how these scripts threaten to engulf their entire sense of self, leaving no vestige of a subjectivity that has not already been shaped by the alienating forces of everyday life, even in this extraordinary time and place of apocalyptic aftermath. In assessing their verbal and physical routines, we might begin with Adorno's strident claim that

> *Endgame* presents the antithesis to existential philosophy's norm that human beings should be what they are because there is nothing else they can be – the idea that this very self is not the self but a slavish imitation of something that does not exist. (Adorno, 1991, 260)

Perhaps Sartre's most famous example of the imperative to be oneself is that of the café waiter whose 'movement is quick and forward, a little too precise, a little too rapid' as he approaches his customers and 'bends forward a little too eagerly; his voice, his eyes express an interest a little too solicitous'. For Sartre, this everyday performance – 'We need not watch for long before we can explain it: he is playing *at being* a waiter' – represents an act of 'bad faith' because, rather than being authentically himself, the waiter has conformed entirely to the social and professional scripts assigned to him (Sartre, 1956, 59). Responding to Sartre's scenario in the opening pages of *Critique of Everyday Life, Volume I*, Lefebvre provides a means for us to understand this dispute, dialectically, in relation to everyday life: 'the waiter in a café is not playing at being a waiter. He is one. And he is not one'. He argues that the act of 'playing' a role allows the waiter to transcend his identity as a waiter, because he is simultaneously defined by and detached from his social function. 'A role is not a role', he claims: 'it is social life and an inherent part of it' (Lefebvre, 2002, 37). This duality suggests a pervasive feature of late capitalist society, where 'each individual exists socially only by and within his alienation, just as he can be for himself and by his deprivation'. It is not too simplistic to suggest that we 'tear off the masks and shatter the roles', nor it is too cynical to say that 'faces are nothing but masks' (38). But Lefebvre still claims that these roles create a familiarity and present a reality: 'masks cling to our faces, to our skin; flesh and blood have become masks' (37).

For Clov, the routines that occupy much of the play are closely associated with his role as a caregiver to Hamm, which takes on the qualities of what Michael Hardt calls 'affective labour' (Hardt, 1999, 89). The 'shelter' that houses the pair is not just a semblance of a home but also a workplace for Clov, where other social and economic relationships may have been stripped away, but the centrality of vocational duties and workaday activity somehow persists. With a distinct air of superiority, Hamm commands him not just to play lookout but to open the windows, to fetch the gaff, to bring his painkiller, to move his chair around the room and so on:

CLOV: Do this, do that, and I do it. I never refuse. Why?
HAMM: You're not able to.
CLOV: Soon I won't do it any more.
HAMM: You won't be able to any more. (*Exit Clov.*) Ah the creatures, everything has to be explained to them. (Beckett, 1986, 113)

Clov can periodically retreat into his kitchen, but he has little opportunity to satisfy any intellectual or social desires, though with little or no civilisation remaining beyond the walls of the shelter the occasions or requirements for these seem to have been cancelled as well. He is in danger of becoming completely consumed by his professional role and yet he clings to the contradictions that would make him something else: a son, a friend, perhaps even a free agent or master. In this sense, his everyday life, far from being outside history, is thoroughly conditioned by the social and economic specificities of its time and place, as strange and estranging as they may be. Moreover, much like Mr Knott's estate, the secluded setting of the shelter highlights the ways in which domestic servitude of this kind can isolate individuals, since it is carried out in a way that divides workers from each other, individualises their burdens and hides their needs from the outside world.

What most clearly distinguishes Clov's form of work are his efforts to manage or modify Hamm's emotional experiences. As Hardt points out, this form of affective labour has a long history, often associated with the undervalued care work of marginalised women, but it has become increasingly central to modern economies since the emergence of late capitalism after the Second World War. Beckett extrapolates this emergent trend to an economy in which it becomes not just a form of labour 'generalized through wide sectors of the economy' but the only form of labour (Hardt, 1999, 97). In doing so, he highlights the emotional dissonance that affective labourers experience in having to perform emotions that do not align with their own feelings; he also emphasises the lack of autonomy that these labourers have when they possess little control over how to express themselves – both conditions, we have noted, exacerbated by the fact that Clov is all but trapped in his domestic setting, with virtually no other opportunities for personal connection or gainful employment. Clov enters the final tableau 'dressed for the road' – that is, for a new role – but he fails to depart as Hamm finishes his final monologue, suggesting his inability to ever abandon his role as caregiver (Beckett, 1986, 132). His judgement of the situation and his motives in this moment remain unspoken, so that his subjectivity is almost entirely opaque, even if we can plainly see that he has reached a moment of decision. As Clov stands there, in this space of lingering aftermath, we know that his labour has been dedicated to the maintenance of sociality, of what persists of society itself, and he cannot yet leave behind that role. The image of Clov that closes the play thus becomes an embodied contradiction, but rather than seeing the play as investigating some existential predicament or metaphysical quandary, we can view it as inquiring into modes of everyday alienation.

This reading is supported by Clov's use of the alarm clock, that essential item for everyday life, which here becomes yet another prompt for its defamiliarisation. The object carries with it a certain ironic charge, since its function in structuring quotidian experience hardly seems necessary in the circumstances of permanent devastation we witness onstage. Its presence would seem to support, even to playfully literalise, existential interpretations of the play as an allegory of 'time-as-death'. If setting an alarm can be seen as part of a typical daily ritual, imposing a regularity and predictability on the temporal flow, it also serves as a reminder of the finite nature of human life. The play humorously affirms this connection when the alarm clock is introduced as a means to let Hamm know if Clov is dead or gone, should the older man's whistles fail to fetch the younger man. But we might counter that Beckett's plays tend to trouble symbolic meaning. In the environment of aftermath on stage, the object also serves as a reminder of a world ordered by the capitalist imperatives of labour, schedules and associated routines that somehow maintain a hold over everyday life, much like the cuckoo-clock had in the opening pages of *Murphy* (even as the clock recalls, more faintly, how these routines have disrupted the natural rhythms of cyclic time). This function was later heightened in *Happy Days*, where Beckett replaced the alarm clock found in early drafts with a prison bell in the final draft. As S. E. Gontarski notes in his study of the play's manuscripts, while Winnie 'regulated her action with the alarm clock, she retained a certain freedom of choice; she could conceivably choose not to respond to the gentle summons of the alarm' (Gontarski, 1977, 38). Instead, the bell rings 'piercingly' and again 'more piercingly' a total of six times during the course of the play, each time to wake up Winnie or to prevent her from dozing off (Beckett, 1986, 138). In *Endgame*, the alarm clock presents one final irony: as Clov readies to leave the shelter, he takes the timepiece down from its hook on the wall and looks for another place to put it, finally setting it down on the ashbin where Nagg has died some time ago. This might be seen as a gesture towards taking control of his routine and even denying the force of clock time and Hamm's authority to regulate his daily rhythms. Yet if Nagg's time has already run out, then by abandoning the clock with him, Clov's opportunity to heed a wake-up call, to release himself from the relentless cycle of servitude and labour, and to transform the conditions of his quotidian existence, may have been abandoned as well.

3 Negativity and Happiness: *Happy Days*

Too often the pared-down aesthetic of Beckett's mature work has been read as the indication of an author who was unconcerned with historical and political matters and was rather concerned with the human condition in some general sense. Such interpretations, as we have seen, often locate his work in a process of abstraction that somehow eludes the binding circumstances of capitalist modernity and yet also alludes to the metaphysical absurdity of human existence in an era characterised by the aftermath of Auschwitz and the escalation of the Cold War. Lukács took issue with Beckett because the critic saw the writer as an example of a modernist whose formal experimentation represented a retreat from social reality, repudiating any engagement with historical struggle and instead promulgating an increasingly decadent bourgeois ideology. For Lukács, the only proper role for artists was to obtain an objective point of view that allowed them to see the totality of society in relation to concrete historical conditions and then to communicate this perspective to others. In Beckett, however, he identified the '*ne plus ultra*' of bourgeois modernism because his work brought its rejection of reality, its escape into nothingness and the associated flight into psychopathology to a 'a glorification of the abnormal' in 'an image of the utmost human degradation' (Lukács, 1963, 32). It was not so much that Beckett and other modernists were wrong in understanding that psychopathology offered a refuge from their historical circumstances but that their writing could not mount a protest against their social conditions, because those social conditions had no prominent place in their writing. Even worse, in Beckett's writing, the flight into psychopathology became 'an immutable *condition humaine*' that offered no possibility of personal or social transformation (31).

In the opening section of *Critique of Everyday Life, Volume II*, Lefebvre alludes to this reading of Beckett as he lays the foundations for the philosophical and sociological inquiry into the quotidian that follows. Here, Lefebvre rejects descriptions of everyday life that focus on the 'small, humble, and sordid side of all human existence' that have 'been part of the everyday since time began' and thus present 'it as timeless and unchangeable' (Lefebvre, 2002, 336–7). If this were the case, he argues, the critique of everyday life would simply bring the most trivial and repellent aspects of social practice to the fore, concentrating on suffering and 'the sordid side of life':

> It would use [...] the stammering, desperate lyricism of a Samuel Beckett as a means of understanding social man. If this were the only path it followed, critique of everyday life would be barely distinguishable from a certain branch of existentialism which took it upon itself – and very skilfully – to underline the marginal elements of existence. (338)

For Lefebvre, this would be a pointless endeavour. Against such sterility, he positions his own sociological criticism, based on the assertion that 'it is in everyday life and starting from everyday life that genuine *creations* are achieved, those creations which produce the human and which men produce as part of the process of becoming human'. At this point in his inquiry, what is most important about 'works of creativity' is that the images, ideas or emotions they produce can be confirmed on the level of quotidian experience, which mediates between culture and the social totality (338; emphasis in original). Much like Lukács, he dismisses Beckett from this program because the writer is seen to reflect little more than the boredom and despair of late capitalist society, rather than to offer a critical perspective on such futility, from which something new might emerge.

In *Critique of Everyday Life, Volume III*, published some two decades after the previous volume, Lefebvre revisits these considerations via his assessment of the concept of modernity and its relation to modern art. Addressing Lukács by name, he notes that for the critic 'modernity and its idolatry accompanied the decline of the bourgeois, its decay as a class was once in the ascendant and sufficiently bold to envisage the universalization of its concepts, values and norms' – and 'the works of the decline [that is, modern art and literature] bear its stamp' (Lefebvre, 2002, 723). But cutting short his 'evocation of this indictment', Lefebvre turns to 'another renowned Marxist theoretician, Adorno', for whom 'modern art possesses aesthetic significance and real value'. It is not that modern art somehow emerges from a source beyond its historical context but that such works are 'the negative moments of their age, marking out the transformations of society and the world'. Examples of what Lefebvre calls 'constructive deconstruction', such works render the unfolding of the historical process visible and intelligible, precisely by employing those aesthetic features that Lukács had condemned: 'the systematic use of ugliness (from Baudelaire to Beckett) and its transformation into formal splendour through appropriate technique – the absence of content and meaning, approximating to emptiness and nothingness [...] and so on'. For Lefebvre, 'the debate between these two interpretations of modernity will remain inconclusive', depending 'in part on the place allotted the negative in dialectical activity'. But in evoking this debate, he nonetheless acknowledges the value of 'Adorno's position' and raises the possibility that 'the negative movement creates something new, that it summons and develops its seeds by dissolving what exists' (723).

This acknowledgement opens the way to employing Lefebvre's philosophy, along with Adorno's, to consider Beckett's mid-career writing as a form of political art addressed to the common, the mundane, the everyday, even as his work leaves behind many of the concrete details of social reality. In this way, his writing can be said to generate a productive negativity through which it defamiliarises the content of everyday life and thus gestures towards the need for alternatives to the status quo. In *Critique of Everyday Life, Volume I*, Lefebvre had noted something of this capacity in Brecht's theatre, which 'perceived the epic content of everyday life' and attached to it 'an acute awareness of the alienation to be found in this same everyday life'. This perception led to theatrical forms that allowed his audience a certain distance from the events on stage, thus making apparent the 'many-sided strangeness' of everyday life and clarifying its inherent contradictions, in which lie the truth of alienation

(Lefebvre, 2002, 42). For Lefebvre, the consciousness of this truth conjured in Brecht's epic theatre had the effect, or at least the potential, of liberating his audiences from their alienation. But for Adorno, the assumption that a work of art could be so thoroughly in possession of its content was little more than a naïve form of empiricism (verging on didacticism and tendentiousness) and marked 'the foreseeable limit of Brecht's work' (Adorno, 1997, 27). Instead, in Adorno's view, the potential identified in Brecht's overtly political writing is better realised in works of art that have previously been described as apolitical because they strive towards autonomy; Brecht's work thus becomes the counterpoint to Beckett's insofar as the latter's writing refuses to affirm any positive content or disalienating message.

For Adorno, Beckett's work is nonetheless deeply political, precisely because it refuses to offer a positive vision of a utopia that somehow transcends the increasing administered and reified world from which it emerges. To its final lines, *Endgame* cannot name the hope that lurks within its pervasive gloom because to do so would be to short-circuit the unnamed power that generates this hope. We might see this as a feature, perhaps the defining feature, of Beckett's late modernism. While his writing is committed to producing heterotopian spaces that provide a critical distance from reigning norms and ideologies, it does not assume the achievement of artistic autonomy or aesthetic detachment; rather, the negotiation of such autonomy becomes a central aesthetic concern. Beckett's art provides a critical knowledge of everyday life not through direct representation but by exploring the ways that everyday life interrogates the possibility of meaning – or, to put this another way, the elusiveness of the everyday is expressed in the elusiveness of Beckett's art. In the process, his writing does not jettison its historical circumstances entirely, it does not leave behind social reality completely, but rather it shows us, precisely in and through its negativity, how capitalist modernity has degraded and deformed humanity.

Concluding his discussion of the 'unresolved controversy' between the perspectives of Lukács and Adorno, Lefebvre suggests that, looking back on the post-war period, 'modernity appears as an ideology' that promised nothing other than 'Happiness, the satisfaction of all needs. This *promesse de bonheur –* no longer through beauty, but by technical means – was to be realized in daily life' (Lefebvre, 2002, 723–4). From this perspective, the most durable feature of modernity is the general movement from the concreteness of nature to 'the abstract-concrete as the mode of social existence, something that extends to works of art' (724). Lefebvre reiterates the now familiar Marxist thesis that the expansion of the world of commodities and the extension of the power of capital find a parallel in movement away from realist and representational forms towards artistic abstraction: 'The artwork thus renounces its previous status: proximity to, and even imitation of, nature' (724). Elsewhere, as we have seen, he defends the critical potential of Brecht's theatre, Joyce's fiction and the work of other modernist writers of the everyday, though here Lefebvre emphasises the degree to which the artwork has become intertwined with and even complicit in the abstracting logic of capitalism. But, in considering Beckett's theatre in relation to the promise of happiness and its association with everyday life, we might turn again to its abstracting tendencies as a mode of negativity, which offer a potential means to critique quotidian experience and its alienating effects. Although Beckett's art and Lefebvre's philosophy approach these concerns from very different positions, it is around the ideology of modernity in the 1960s that their interests clearly converge.

Perhaps this is most evident in Beckett's last full-length play, *Happy Days*. The drama centres on Winnie, whose actions follow a repetitive pattern of quotidian self-care: she brushes her teeth, combs her hair, polishes her spectacles, applies her lipstick, files her nails, takes her medicine, inspects herself in a mirror and so on. She accompanies these mundane activities with idle chatter, an almost ceaseless stream of worn-out words, sometimes directed at her husband, Willie, and sometimes directed, it seems, at no one in particular. Although he seldom answers and she worries that often 'words fail', Winnie keeps up the banter, just as she keeps up her grooming regimen, resorting when necessary to repeating advertising slogans or reiterating tired clichés (Beckett, 1986, 147). When Willie responds, if he responds at all, she can expect little more than 'titbits' read out from *Reynolds' News* (167). All this might appear to be completely ordinary, mundane, were it not for the extraordinary setting the characters inhabit on stage: '*Expanse of scorched grass rising centre to low mound. Gentle slopes down to front and either side of stage. Back an abrupter fall to stage level. Maximum of simplicity and symmetry. Blazing light*' (138). Sunk into the mound up to her waist and then up to her neck, the figure of Winnie completes the remarkable tableau. 'In this play', Beckett once explained, 'you have a combination of the strange and the practical, the mysterious and the factual', a combination that highlights the elusive quality of the everyday, even as it makes the quotidian vivid in a way that realist modes of representation seldom do (qtd in Fehsenfeld, 1987, 54).

The play renounces imitation of or proximity to a particular social reality, but it retains an oblique relationship with the defining characteristics of modernity. In a sense, *Happy Days* takes place beyond the end of history, in the wastelands that persist after our institutions and their edifices have crumbled. These are landscapes that impose a stark image of the failures of modernity upon the audience: rather than material abundance and technological prowess, they present us with a world stripped or nearly stripped of all signs of civilisation. Yet somehow the everyday persists. These are not metaphors for some absolute state of being so much as inquiries into how daily life must be experienced in such circumstances, which the characters struggle to fill with repetitive behaviours: 'What *is* one to do? [...] All day long. [...] Day after Day.', Winnie wonders (Beckett, 1986, 156). The spectre of boredom lingers in these evacuated spaces. Like Hamm and Clov, Winnie and Willie persist after some catastrophe has rendered their world worldless, giving place to forms of alienation that suggest a critical response to the social and economic conditions of post-war Europe. As we have noted, France in particular had experienced a rapid transformation of domestic life, profoundly influenced by a consumerist ideology introduced in the 1950s and 1960s. Historians of everyday life have often remarked on the unprecedented speed of modernisation, with its shifts in culture and consumption, with its new refrigerators and telephones, washing machines and automobiles, spurred on by American financial support aimed at restoring the French economy.[10] Over the course of the two decades, the mainstream of French society was swept up in this ideology, to the point that everyday life itself seemed dependent on 'the presentation which the bourgeoisie has and makes us have of the relations between man and the world' (Barthes, 2013, 252). Given this, we might view *Happy Days* as tearing down the walls of the newly modernised domestic interiors, where the middle classes in France, England and elsewhere in Europe had withdrawn after the war, to expose them to harsh inspection under the relentless light of the sun.

In their strange context, the objects in Winnie's handbag provide us with an image of this new phase of capitalism even as these consumer products provide some order and orientation to her quotidian experience. The bag itself is an object that reinforces traditional gender roles in the face of rapid social and economic changes insofar as such an accessory was seen as essential for a woman in maintaining her personal appearance and in organising her family life.[11] The everyday items kept in the bag – the toothbrush, the comb, the spectacles, the lipstick, the nail file, the medicine, the mirror – are all associated with the many self-care rituals she undertakes through the course of her day. They offer themselves as convenient tools for avoiding boredom and finding happiness. Applying her lipstick, for instance, Winnie participates in an everyday activity that links her situation with both the glamour of Hollywood actresses and the expansion of popular brands such as Revlon and Max

---

[10] See, for instance, Ross (1996, 1997, 2023).

[11] See Bates for an extended discussion of the contents of Winne's bag and the ways that these items determine the course of the play (2017, 174–9).

Factor. The cosmetic is a small token of the upheavals in social and economic relations that have taken place in the world beyond the evacuated stage, where consumer imperatives have now permeated the deepest recesses of private life and the very rhythms of quotidian existence. The largest of her props, a parasol, offers Winnie some modicum of use value, by providing her protection from the harsh sun above. But it also gestures towards the feminine attributes of grace and decorum, while indicating her adherence to standards of beauty that prized fairness and delicacy above all else. To the extent that Winnie repeats familiar rituals with familiar props, day after day, she is transformed into a kind of automaton and, in this sense, the objects suggest something about the force of both consumer culture and the familiar social scripts assigned to Winnie as woman and wife (however unfamiliar the rituals and props may now appear amid her current situation).

The situation on stage also draws attention more intently to the quality of her speech, which has become just as repetitive and ritualised as her behaviour. In general, Winnie speaks simply to contend with the slow movement of the hours and the days. Her speech is largely characterised by routine phrases and expressions, repeated over and over, thus losing their expressive quality in the seemingly endless cycle of her quotidian existence. But, again, what Beckett presents to us is less a reiteration of 'everyday speech' than a metalanguage addressed to 'everyday speech', so that we are invited to reflect on this level of discourse. Winnie's monologue opens with the stock phrase 'another heavenly day', which is indicative of a verbal ritual that must commence each new day, no matter how ironic the phrase seems in her infernal surroundings. This is followed by 'an inaudible prayer', which is punctuated with an audible 'for Jesus Christ sake Amen' and concludes with 'World word without end Amen' (Beckett, 1986, 138). Like so many of Winnie's later utterances, even these pious phrases suggest the kind of language that circulates through everyday life without really belonging to anyone in particular and without expressing any individual subjectivity, but instead reflecting the undifferentiated quality of everyday existence.

Much the same could be said of the many quotations and misquotations from various literary sources – Shakespeare, Browning, Gray, Keats, Khayyam, Milton, Yeats and others – that Winnie resorts to throughout her monologue. Ulrika Maude has called these 'manifestations of linguistic automatism' because they 'function here precisely in the manner of culturally coded chants or mantras: they are key lines from Western literature, but their signification, for Winnie, has long since been obliterated' (Maude, 2014, 50). Their reiteration is little more than a verbal habit, which not only warps their original form but also saps them of any semantic content. Her speech is also punctuated by frequent pauses, as many as twenty in a single page of text, which disrupt her train of thought and create a form of speech characterised by fragmentation, incompletion and ambiguity. But, for Winnie, it matters little whether she completely remembers or comprehends her lines. What matters is that they make everyday life bearable for her by assuaging her boredom and her worries and even opening her world to a certain wonder, even if it is in some sense simulated or insensible. For his part, Willie spends much of the play silently reading the newspaper, the textual form most closely associated with the everyday, though, as Lefebvre argues, it is unable to seize on the insignificance of the quotidian because it must repeatedly pronounce it 'sensational'. The newspaper, as Blanchot claims, thus focuses on the anecdote, the 'titbit', to be consumed daily by the reader, and thus, 'having replaced the "nothing happens" of the everyday with the emptiness of the news item', it provides us with an image of history that only further obscures the 'unqualifiable everyday' (Blanchot, 1987, 18).

Winnie's speech is thus not so much a tool for communication as a habitual means to keep herself occupied through the course of her day and, from time to time, to evoke some affirmation of her selfhood from Willie. Her repetition of these borrowed words and phrases, even in her discourse with herself, serves as a reminder of the ways that private consciousness interacts with and is dependent upon public consciousness, with its ready-made explanations, mystifying promises and other compensations. Significantly, this also includes her repetition of the marketing copy inscribed on her toothbrush – 'genuine pure . . . Fully guaranteed . . . ' – several times during the play, which only emphasises how capitalism and its consumerist imperatives penetrate the domain of everyday life and estrange people from themselves. To be sure, Lefebvre attributed his return to the topic of everyday life in the 1960s to the near ubiquity of such language, which he had noted in a particular exchange with his wife: she returned from shopping one day with a box of laundry detergent and, unconsciously mimicking an advertising slogan, announced, '*This* is an excellent product' (Ross, 1997, 22). In an insightful essay on *Happy Days*, Julie Bates has suggested that Winnie's repeated attempts to decipher the inscription indicate her own 'apparent susceptibility to the language of marketing' and contribute to 'Beckett's dismissive association of female characters with products and brands' (Bates, 2019, 55–6). But I would add that the metalinguistic function of the dialogue also draws attention to how the words in the slogan have been detached from any corresponding signified or referent and thus made available for the purposes of advertising: the 'genuine' and 'pure' product that promises to care for the consumer and endow her with whiter-than-white teeth, a 'genuine' and 'pure' smile that will in turn transform her social reality (if only a recognisable social reality remained). The language does not offer a description of the material qualities of the consumer object so much as a fiction framed around the promise of 'happiness' – 'the happiness', as Lefebvre stresses, 'of being a consumer' (Lefebvre, 1971, 105). At the same time, as Winnie struggles to make out the words, she experiences a perpetual insecurity about her happiness, her habitual need to tell herself that 'this is going to be another happy day', which suggests that consumption, whatever comfort, ease, or distraction it might provide, is not the same as happiness (Beckett, 1986, 142).

Lefebvre's critique of everyday life has itself been criticised, and rightly so, for veering into reductive and even misogynistic accounts of women's experience. In *Everyday Life in the Modern World*, he claims that 'everyday life weighs heaviest on women', in part because (as we have just seen) he believed that women are less resistant to its demands or the enticements of consumer society, which targeted their femininity and valued it according to a set of physical qualities: well-brushed teeth, well-combed hair, a well-tended figure and so on. At the same time, he also saw it 'as highly probable that they also get something out of it, by reversing the situation', because, in his estimation, women generally directed consumption in late capitalist societies (Lefebvre, 1971, 73). Perhaps it is only coincidental that, in elaborating on the relationship of women to everyday life, he describes behaviours and draws on imagery that seem to evoke, albeit patronisingly, the manic monologue and striking tableau of *Happy Days*:

> Some are bogged down by its peculiar cloying substance, others escape into make believe, close their eyes to their surroundings, to the bog into which they are sinking and simply ignore it; they have their substitutes and they are substitutes; they complain – about men, the human condition, life, God and the gods – but they are always beside the point; they are the subject of everyday life and its victims or objects and substitutes (beauty, femininity, fashion, etc.) and it is at their cost that substitutes thrive. Likewise they are both buyers and consumers of commodities and symbols for commodities (in advertisements, as nudes and smiles). (73)

The passage, however, demonstrates a major limitation in Lefebvre's project. In describing how women become trapped in and try to escape from everyday life under late capitalism, he suggests that their reliance on 'substitutes' leads them to a debilitating state of false consciousness. Yet in categorising the 'beauty, femininity, fashion, etc.' this way, he only reinforces the patriarchal ideology that commodifies women's experience and women's bodies, rather than recognising and critiquing the ways patriarchal ideology is implicated in consumerist ideology (73). He goes on to claim that 'the ideology of *femininity* or of happiness by and in femininity is only another form of the ideology of consumption (happiness through consuming) and the ideology of technicality (women possessing the technique of happiness!), but with something more appealing' (96; italics in original). While he attempts to reveal how late capitalism commodifies both feminity and happiness, Lefebvre does so in a way that clearly diminishes the agency of women while failing to acknowledge the ways that femininity has been shaped by patriarchal power structures.

In contrast, *Happy Days* can be read as a critique of these power structures and the ways that gender hierarchies and consumerist imperatives work together to shape everyday life. The most salient example of this is found precisely in Winnie's continual puzzling over the advertising slogan on her toothbrush handle, which eventually leads her to the realisation that the phrase in full reads 'genuine pure .... ah! hog's setae', or bristle. Pressing Willie for a definition of 'hog', she evokes a terse response – 'Castrated male swine. (*Happy expression appears on Winnie's face.*) Reared for slaughter' – that, now evoking a subversive joy, suggests an emasculation of the patriarchal regime of consumer capitalist society: 'Oh this is a happy day!', she exclaims (Beckett, 1986, 159). Her exclamation ironically, and thus critically, refigures the very 'happiness through consuming' that Lefebvre critiques by suggesting that her joy comes from sensing, in the banality of everyday language, the very contradictions that shape her experience under this regime.

It is important to note that Beckett refuses to release his audience from such contradictions. By placing Winnie on display at the centre of a barren stage, with 'her arms and shoulders bare, low bodice, big bosom, pearl necklace' (138), the play also offers an implicit rebuke to the spectators in the theatre insofar as they view women as symbols of this consumer happiness, deployed as 'subjects of advertising, nakedness, smiles, living display units' (Lefebvre, 2002, 173). Beckett, moreover, redeploys what Lefebvre calls 'the Smile Myth (the joy of consuming identified with the imaginary joy of the man or woman depicted consuming the object)', as Winnie repeatedly, almost mechanically, switches on her white, well-brushed smile, that 'symbol of everyday happiness', and just as quickly switches it off (Beckett, 1986, 105, 56). In making the performance of feminine happiness so like that of an automaton, so obviously artificial and mechanical, *Happy Days* shows us that such happiness is necessarily manufactured, but it also suggests a more radical critique of the forms of physical and emotional control exerted by patriarchal power structures.

Just how concerned Beckett's writing is with the promise – and the ideology – of happiness, especially during this most productive period of his career, is something that Lefebvre, Lukács and many later critics seem to miss.[12] Adorno, however, recognised that Beckett's work, in exploring the degradation and deformation of the subject, retains the smallest glimmer of hope for happiness, even if it can only be accessed through the starkest renderings of everyday life: 'The minimal promise of happiness which they contain, which refuses to be traded for any consolation, was to be had only at the price of a thoroughgoing articulation, to the point of worldlessness' (Adorno, 1991, 360). If the concern is announced plainly enough in the title of *Happy Days*, the title and the play tend to be read in strictly ironic terms, given the deprived conditions of Winnie's environment, as well as the desperate actions and utterances that form her response to them. But to read the title as merely ironic, a direct contradiction of what we witness on stage, is to overlook the ways that the play, along with *Waiting for Godot* and *Endgame*, concerns the promise of happiness, even (or especially) in the most degrading and degraded circumstances. The heterotopian settings of the plays seem to have always already ruled out the possibility of happiness, and yet some small residuum persists in the everyday activities that continue on even in the aftermath of catastrophe. Winnie, whatever her other confusions and uncertainties, is nonetheless sure that she wants happiness, whether that comes in the form of recognition from her husband, some sign of her own vitality, or the mere hope of something better. *Waiting for Godot* raises the question of happiness repeatedly: in relation to Estragon's former dreams of happiness, to the sociability that the tramps briefly enjoy with Pozzo, to the master's sadistic reign over his slave, then his joy at eating and drinking hardily ('Happy days!'), to the various efforts the two tramps make to assure each other that they are indeed happy or were at some point, and finally, perhaps most touchingly, to Estragon's fleeting dream that he was happy. In *Endgame*, Hamm may assert that 'nothing is funnier than unhappiness', but that also suggests the corollary of this claim, that nothing is more tragic than happiness, or at least the expectations and illusions of happiness.

These plays thus conduct an inquiry not into some 'immutable *condition humaine*' but into the promise of happiness in relation to the perpetual crisis of modernity and its constant mutilation to subjectivity. Winnie's future-perfect 'this will have been a happy day' suggests both a pathos-ridden optimism about the possibility of achieving happiness in these conditions and an oppressive modern imperative to pursue happiness at any cost (Beckett, 1986, 155). Modern subjects have been taught to expect happiness from their consumption,

---

[12] The one book-length study of happiness in Beckett's writing, David Kleinberg-Levin's *Beckett's Words: The Promise of Happiness in a Time of Mourning* (2015), draws on Adorno (along many other philosophers), but primarily focuses on aesthetics, formal innovation and the phenomenology of language, divorced from specific historical or material concerns.

their leisure, their everyday life, but this ideology conceals the alienating forces of late capitalist society. This is not to suggest that Beckett's texts contain some hidden key to happiness for his readers or spectators. His writing does not offer even the most tenuous instructions for self-help or some alternative technique of happiness, even or especially through art. Rather, in its productive negativity, it works to disrupt the ideology of happiness and to critique those elements of late capitalist culture and society that exploit that ideology in everyday life. The force of this negativity suggests that our happiness cannot be turned into a form of praxis or a mode of labour. Rather than enticing us to participate in any such utopian illusion, which would distract us from the brute fact that we are always already embedded (up to our necks, as it were) in the socio-political conditions of everyday life, he invites us to witness the conditions that have created our servitude and alienation even as he begins prying open an alternative space of possibility.

4 The Terrorism of Everyday Life: *Rough for Theatre II*, *The Lost Ones* and *Rockaby*

Beckett's inquiry into the ideology of happiness continues in *Rough for Theatre II*, begun 'circa 1960' but not published until 1976.[13] The play features two civil servants – A (Bertrand) and B (Morvan) – seated at tables in an otherwise empty flat, as they discuss the contents of a '*briefcase crammed with documents*' in order to determine whether a third man – C (Croker) – should jump from a nearby window, at which he stands for the duration of the drama (Beckett, 1986, 237). The examination of the documents yields details about C's physiological ailments, his psychological needs, phobias and sensitivities, as well as his difficult boyhood and romantic history. Building their case, the bureaucrats effectively 'sum up' the life of this unfortunate individual from what amounts to bureaucratic data, derived from official records and third-party testimony: 'we have been to the best sources. All weighed and weighed again, checked and verified' (238). The first piece of documentation that they examine – the testimony of C's wife, Mrs Aspasia Budd-Croker – yields a picture of pathos and disaffection:

> 'Questioned on this occasion'—open brackets—'(judicial separation)'—close brackets— 'regarding the deterioration of our relations, all he could adduce was the five or six miscarriages which clouded'—open brackets '(oh through no act of mine!)'—close brackets—'the early days of our union and the veto which in consequence I had finally to oppose'—open brackets—'(oh not for want of inclination!)'—close brackets—'to anything remotely

---

[13] Cited in this Element via Beckett (1986).

resembling the work of love. But on the subject of our happiness'—open brackets—'(for it too came our way, unavoidably, and here my mind goes back to the first vows exchanged at Wooton Bassett under the bastard acacias, or again to the first fifteen minutes of our wedding night at Littlestone-on-Sea, or yet again to those first long studious evenings in our nest on Commercial Road East)'—close brackets—'on the subject of our happiness not a word, Sir, not one word'. (239–40)

Such disappointments might be read as an absurdist rendering of *la condition humaine*, made up of one personal tragedy after another to the point that suffering seems inevitable and happiness becomes unspeakable. The scenario of the play evokes Albert Camus' famed contention at the outset of *The Myth of Sisyphus* – that 'there is but one truly serious philosophical problem, and that is suicide. Judging whether life is or is not worth living amounts to answering the fundamental question of philosophy' – but transforms into a bureaucratic concern (Camus, 1955, 3). The mediation of the testimony through the administrative process that unfolds in the play has the effect of satirising both the mythic pretensions of Existential philosophy and the institutional logic that might judge a human life based on a bureaucratic evaluation of such materials. If C is to have the lucidity to see his life without self-deception (the kind of lucidity that, for Camus, provides Sisyphus some happiness in the end), he will, quite ironically, have to rely on the efforts of these two civil servants to provide it for him. That C remains entirely silent throughout this process suggests just how thoroughly his subjectivity has been effaced by the functioning of the bureaucratic apparatus, which isolates, objectifies and alienates him as it scrutinises the external facts of his life according to a process over which he seemingly has no influence.

The heterotopian space in which the play takes place compounds the sense that bureaucracy has infiltrated virtually every corner of everyday life and its lived environments. The sparsely decorated stage space – comprising a '*high double window open on the sky*' upstage, two small tables with chairs downstage audience left and downstage audience right, and a door downstage left – is evidently the current habitation of C, though we are told that 'this is not his home. He's only here to take care of the cat' (Beckett, 1986, 237, 239). We also learn that this anonymous abode, virtually devoid of personal effects or family mementos, is located on the sixth floor or higher of an apartment building, meaning that it is just one among many similar habitations on the surrounding floors. Unlike the heterotopian spaces of *Happy Days*, *Endgame*, or even *Waiting for Godot*, there is nothing particularly extraordinary about the world of *Rough for Theatre II* and the play does not aspire to create an entirely separate sphere. What makes the space unhomely is the presence of the civil servants, who infiltrate this ostensibly private domain to carry out their bureaucratic process of assessing the life of this individual.

This is, in other words, a space where everyday life is in intimate contact with the State and its efforts to administer society in the name of order, control and moral discipline, efforts that Lefebvre calls 'the insignia of terrorist societies' (Lefebvre, 1971, 161). For the philosopher, terrorist societies have little to do with political violence; rather, they have to do with the evolution of consumer societies into repressive structures that are maintained through both ideological persuasion and various forms of compulsion, including laws and codes, police and bureaucrats. The presence of the civil servants in *Rough for Theatre II* transforms a domestic space into a gloomy microcosm of the totally administered world. The power of the written word, which Lefebvre associates closely with 'terrorist societies', knows no limitations here as bureaucratic rationality based on written matter seeks to penetrate the deepest recesses of everyday life. This rationality exerts its pressure on C at every level of his experience and background. But the terror (and, to be sure, the dark humour too) of all this is most forceful in the visual irony of the situation on stage: a man stands on a precipice, apparently contemplating his own death, while two bureaucrats fumble through their official documents and largely ignore the vulnerable human being so near them. The image graphically displays the degree to which bureaucracy has become a self-enclosed system, operating for and by itself; A and B embody this dehumanising bureaucratic function, which, as Lefebvre writes, 'integrates people by turning them into bureaucrats (thus training them for the bureaucratic administration of their own daily lives) and rationalises "private" life to its own standards' (159).

Beckett's heterotopian fictions can be regarded as articulating the persistent anxiety and alienation of everyday life in 'a modern formally "free society"' through a mode of writing that radically defamiliarises social reality. It is for this reason, in large part, that Slavoj Žižek has called Beckett '*the* great writer of abstraction', despite the fact that, as he acknowledges, for a partisan of conventional Marxist historical analysis like Lukács, Beckett's abstraction cannot but appear as resolutely '"anti-Marxist"' (Žižek, 2019, 454). For Žižek, on the other hand,

> when he depicts the subjective experience of terror, loss, suffering and persecution, he does not endeavour to locate it in a concrete historical context (say, making it clear that it is a moment of Fascist terror in an occupied country, or of the Stalinist terror against dissident intellectuals). (454)

Beckett does something entirely, or almost entirely, contradictory: he places specific forms of terror into a continuum that creates 'an abstract and de-contextualized terror', one can even say Platonic terror (454). Drawing on the work of Emilie Morin, Žižek reads Beckett's late play, *Catastrophe* – with its minimalist set directions: '*Rehearsal. Final touches to last scene. Bare stage*' (Beckett, 1986, 457) – as an allegory not just of 'the power of totalitarianism and the struggle to oppose it, the protagonist representing people ruled by dictators (the director and his aide)' (qtd in Žižek, 2019, 456), but, in its metatheatrical mode, as an indictment of the theatre audience for 'enjoying the spectacle of suffering which makes you feel good in your solidarity with the victim' (457). What Beckett allows us to see, in writing that moves towards abstraction but never arrives at a completely ahistorical remove, is not a set of concrete material conditions but a series of shifting historical possibilities – modes of power, of suffering, of victimhood – that blurs their distinctions and reconstructs each of them in an *almost* entirely abstract and idealised form. For Žižek, Beckett's negation of historical specificity reveals both the psychological truth of the victim and the ontological truth of the social totality, in a manner that surpasses the '"concrete" realist image of social totality' (454).

In these circumstances, it may seem that Beckett's beleaguered characters have little to do with political critique and yet, as Žižek points out, they function in part as 'political metonymies' (Žižek, 2019, 454). As we can discern in *Rough for Theatre II*, the political order they inhabit begins to show itself, to 'materialise', precisely through their encounters with forms of terror that largely elude direct representation or categorisation. At A's prompting, B searches in the documents for an example of the 'positive elements' of C's life story and then reads from 'that incident of the lottery':

> 'Two hundred lots ... winner receives high class watch ... solid gold, hallmark nineteen carats, marvel of accuracy, showing year, month, date, day, hour, minute and second, super chic, unbreakable hair spring, chrono escapement nineteen rubies, anti-shock, anti-magnetic, airtight, waterproof, stainless, self-winding, centre seconds hand, Swiss parts, deluxe lizard band' (Beckett, 1986, 240–1).

Again, as in *Endgame*, the mention of the timepiece and its timekeeping capacity suggest Existentialist themes regarding the experience of duration and the inevitability of death. Of course, it also indicates a connection with everyday life insofar as it tracks the units of time that make up the cycles of daily existence and supports capitalist imperatives of schedules, labour and associated routines. But this passage, with its heightened marketing language – 'high class', 'super chic': deluxe' and so on – also exceeds such interpretations insofar as it endows the object with signs of wealth and class, value and luxury, to present us with a desirable consumer object and its implicit promises of pleasure and happiness (along with the reifying and alienating effects that consumer products have on both human activities and human beings).

It should also be noted that this language comes from an advertisement for a sweepstake, which asks ticket buyers to chance their luck in the hope of attaining such a desirable object. Part of the irony of this passage resides in the fact that, as we soon learn, C did not buy the ticket himself but rather received it (or did not refuse it) as a gift. In that regard, it suggests only the faintest glimmer of optimism. In his radical quietism (much like Murphy before him), C has tried to opt out of the capitalist enterprise and what Lefebvre calls 'the pleasure economy', with its capacity to arouse needs and desires, many of which would nevertheless remain unsatisfied. Later in the play, A wonders about the files: 'Is there a single reference there to personal gain?' (Beckett, 1986, 246). That the watch, this desirable object, is implicated in a scheme dependent on luck, rather than skill, hard work and so forth, suggests something more fundamental about the pleasure economy:

> Satisfaction is characterized by accident and contingency. It is a 'stroke of good fortune', a windfall, a piece of luck. In so far as the words mean anything, joy and happiness consist of a series of favourable encounters and chances. Freedom, so frequently exalted, is not more than the skill of making the most of luck and chance. (Lefebvre, 2002, 367)

Thus, C opts out, or attempts to opt out, not only from the link between satisfaction and consumer goods but also from the ideology that would celebrate good luck in the instance of an individual man and his social reality. One is seen as lucky because he wins a gold watch, but this does not take into account how improved forms of social organisation might have given him a better chance of happiness from the beginning.

As much as any of Beckett's work, *Rough for Theatre II* demonstrates how the insistent unfreedom and terror of late capitalist society can be illuminated by writing that avoids direct realist representation of that society. For C to elude his own chance at happiness seems to be tantamount not just to the individual or psychological concern of opting out of happiness but to a more general concern of opting out of the capitalist enterprise (and perhaps life altogether). Later, we hear the testimony of a Mr Feckman, who recounts the last time he saw C as the former was on his way to the post office to cash a cheque for back-pay. 'To all appearances down and out', C sat on a bench with his head down, scrutinising a lump of dogshit with great intensity, otherwise insensate to and uninvolved with the world around him. Mr Feckman notes that this strange activity continued from three o'clock in the afternoon until at least two hours later, when C might well have been at some form of employment. Not having the heart to greet C and perhaps disrupt his strange meditation, Mr Feckman instead slips a lottery ticket into his pocket, as if to offer him an invitation back to the world of getting and spending. But C remains in his nearly catatonic state, unmoved by the gesture.

Is this an image of radical alienation? Or a radical critique of late capitalism, substituting fascination with a lump of dog shit for commodity fetishism? C stands at the window, with his back to the audience, throughout the course of the play (apparently overhearing the civil servants at work and contemplating his own death), though we learn eventually that he has 'that little smile on his face'. For the civil servants, the smile is an enigmatic sign that disrupts their interpretation of C's pathetic life story and throws their bureaucratic narrative into doubt: 'Could never make out what he thought he was doing with that smile on his face' (Beckett, 1986, 245). Is this the sign of a retreat into psychopathology, precipitated by the painful absurdities of his life story or by the damaging forces of late capitalist society more generally? Or is it, much like Winnie's smile, a sign of resistance to the social scripts that, in this case, would assign this unfortunate man to his impending fate? Of his final resignation to that fate? Of 'the minimal promise of happiness'? At the very least, the enigmatic smile suggests that something, some kind of residuum, has managed to escape the efforts of bureaucrats to conclusively assess, organise and manage every facet of quotidian existence, despite their best efforts. All we learn at the end of the play, when A goes to inspect C again, is that his expression has changed in some remarkable way: 'Take a look at this! ... Come on! Quick! ... Well I'll be ... !' (Beckett, 1986, 249).

Tasked with assessing such details, the civil servants are effectively assigned to judge the quality of C's everyday life, as 'the realm of the confrontations and distances which the words "good luck" and "bad luck" summarize in a naïve dialectic' (Lefebvre, 2002, 398). The fact that C has failed to attain happiness seems less important than the meaning of his failure and what can be learnt from the quality of his missteps. The bureaucrats pore over the more or less trivial specifics of his life story in a vain effort to identify something more profound, to see if C's many social failures might be indicative of positive qualities: '(independent thinking, critical intelligence, rebellion)' and so forth (399). They must make a judgement based on the collection of problems, contradictions and possibilities that add up to the 'person' before them, a collection that promises to demonstrate the value of this individual in some way. 'Here', says B, slapping his pile of papers, 'as far as I'm concerned the client is here and nowhere else' (Beckett, 1986, 246). Of course, as they read out the details, they implicate members of the theatre audience in the same process, inviting, even prompting us to pass judgement on this individual based on the snippets of the bureaucratic archive offered to us. But (and this is perhaps the crux of the brief play) the two of them – 'men like us', as A says – demonstrate that they have been trained for the bureaucratic administration of their own lives, which rationalises their private experience according to its own administrative standards (237). It seems that A is more humane than the rather callous B, but both civil servants see their efforts as a mere job, to be concluded in time to pack up and catch the evening train to their next destination and their next appointment. What pity they can muster is reserved for the dead finch they discover in a cage as the play comes to an end. If their shared bureaucratic conscience becomes a general social conscience in the play, their work exhibits the pervasive power of modern bureaucracy for the audience and demonstrates the ways that it spreads terror through everyday life.

In prose, Beckett's art of abstraction reaches an apotheosis of sorts in *The Lost Ones*, with its stark vision of a radically administered society of ceaseless everyday terrors. Less a narrative than a description of a strange heterotopian space and a series of social arrangements, the text begins with language that is at once detailed and radically abstracted, offering a thoroughly impoverished image of daily life:

> Abode where lost bodies roam each search for its lost one. Vast enough for search to be in vain. Narrow enough for flight to be in vain. Inside flattened cylinder fifty metres round and sixteen high for the sake of harmony. The light. Its dimness. Its yellowness. Its omnipresence as though every separate square centimetre were agleam of the some twelve million total surface. Its restlessness at long intervals suddenly stilled like panting at the last. Then all go dead still. It is perhaps the end of their above. A few seconds and all begins again. (Beckett, 1995, 202)

Here is a highly organised space where human activity has been reduced to a few elementary relations, all overseen – each curve, niche and tunnel – from the probing perspective of the narrator. In a sense, nothing could be further from everyday experience. Of course, the fictional world constructed, piece by piece, in the pages that follow is one that corresponds to no actual physical space beyond the text. The abstraction of the text has invited a range of allegorical interpretations, including those that evoke the human condition, the authorial situation, the quest for being, the singularisation of the subject and a phenomenology of vision or touch. On the other hand, Lois Oppenheim has called *The Lost Ones* an 'autoconstitutional' text because 'the textual world does not initially present itself in relation to a world outside it' (Oppenheim, 2000, 168). She argues instead that, with its detailed mathematical specifications and overtly constructed images, *The Lost Ones* demonstrates an ontological autonomy that serves to 'remind us that other world configurations are possible' (168).

More recently, critics such as Fintan O'Toole, James Little and James McNaughton have examined the confined space constructed by this idiosyncratic text to elucidate the political dynamics of Beckett's writing.[14] Adding to this work, I would contend that this textual space presents a largely abstract image of a totally administered world, where instrumental rationality and bureaucratic control have infiltrated nearly every aspect of everyday life. Moreover, I would suggest that the text offers a vision of what Lefebvre calls the 'pure (formal) space' that defines the world of terror, where 'so-called human actions and objects are catalogued, classed and tidied away, together with writings that are lined up on written matter' (Lefebvre, 1971, 179). In this regard, *The Lost Ones* parodies and implicitly critiques the 'aspiration to a pure abstraction' that bureaucracy imposes on everyday life in the effort to organise it completely. The narrator – who is often 'cold and determinedly clinical', as Ruby Cohn has suggested – provides us with a generalised account of the behaviour of the inhabitants, rendered in impersonal declarative statements, rather than depictions of specific incidents, actions, or encounters (Cohn, 2005, 309). The inhabitants of the cylinder are divided into four social groups, according to how they seek their 'lost ones': the searchers, those who pause, the sedentary and the vanquished. Despite the abstraction of their situation, they function as 'political metonymies' in their encounters with the highly organised social order that begins to reveal itself as they run up against its restrictions and coercions. Trapped in the cylinder, they conduct their searches in standardised ways, including crawling through a system of tunnels in the walls of the cylinder and climbing a series of ladders placed at intervals around its circumference. The meticulous attention to various protocols – the specific rules for ladder usage, the prescribed waiting periods, the regulated temperature fluctuations and so forth – exemplifies the programming of everyday life, so that all activity in the cylinder incessantly serves to reproduce existing social relations. Although the narrative perspective is authoritative enough to foretell the fate of the inhabitants, even if they have no sense of it themselves, the narrator at times slips into errors, inconsistencies and uncertainties. As we will see, it is precisely in these inconsistencies that the protocols of the cylinder fail to organise the everyday completely, that something escapes, that some residual remains.

---

[14] See O'Toole (2018), Little (2020, 3) and McNaughton (2024, 23–34).

But first, let us look more closely at the world constructed by the text. Beckett's biographers have suggested that the enclosed space and regimented behaviours of its inhabitants were inspired by La Santé Prison, which he could observe from the window of his Parisian apartment. Indeed, *The Lost Ones* can be read as a meditation on the conditions of the incarcerated, as well as a reflection on the fate of inmates in a concentration camp or, by the late 1960s, an inquiry into the operation of power in everyday life in modern formally free societies. Yet the historical possibilities presented by the text can be condensed into the more inclusive idea of the oppression of total social administration in a society where, as Lefebvre describes it, 'terror is diffuse, violence is always latent, pressure is exerted from all sides on its members' (Lefebvre, 1971, 147). The anonymous figures who circulate through the narrative become interchangeable victims of a totalising or nearly totalising force, embodied in the all-encompassing architecture of the heterotopian space they inhabit. This architecture provides an image of heterotopia as a kind of technocratic dystopia, where the ordering of space, without regard for lived experience, creates a site of pervasive alienation rather than emergent liberation. Transforming the social relations and human experiences in this space, creating some utopian hope, would most certainly require prying open a gap of freedom, if not demolishing its architecture and fashioning an entirely new one, without the mechanisms of control that define the cylinder.

In a sense, then, we are presented with a world that is an extrapolation of the repressive capitalist societies that developed during the twentieth century. It manifests an almost absolute mode of what Lefebvre identifies as the dominance of abstract space (with its very concrete constraints) in modern capitalist societies, which is homogenised, controlled and stripped of meaning beyond its mere functionality. The world of *The Lost Ones* conjoins multiple modes of repression into a single suffocating space, where individuals are constrained by a matrix of design and organisational measures. With Lefebvre's theories of spatial production in mind, we can clearly see that this cylindrical world is not merely an empty container, not merely a physical construct but a space socially constructed by the routines and restrictions imposed upon the figures who inhabit it:

> Bodies themselves generate spaces, which are produced by and for their gestures. The linking of gestures corresponds to the articulation and linking of well-defined spatial segments, segments which repeat, but whose repetition gives rise to novelty. [...] Many such social spaces are given rhythm by the gestures which are produced within them, and which produce them (and they are accordingly often measured in paces, cubits, feet, palms or thumbs). The everyday microgestural realm generates its own spaces (for example, footways, corridors, places for eating). (Lefebvre, 1991, 216)

The cylinder is a manifestation of social forces that shape the lives of its inhabitants, who experience a kind of totalitarian control over their movement and behaviour. There is seemingly no room or opportunity, within the radically regimented design of the cylinder, for the tactical reappropriation or spontaneous reconstitution of space, which would allow each citizen and the entire community of the cylinder to spontaneously revise the terms of their everyday life. Compared to the abstract space of the planners, architects, or technocrats responsible for the design of this strange world, the space of the everyday activities of the figures in the cylinder is a concrete or material one, which, as Lefebvre stresses, is subjective. We may feel a kind of sympathy for them, recognising in these structures radicalised forms of our own alienation and repression.

The hyperbole of restrictions, prescriptions and confinements suggests a clearer vision, perhaps even a Platonic form, of the oppressive structures that underpin late capitalist society. But Beckett subtly undermines the system and its function each time uncertainties creep into the textual construction of the cylinder. As Cohn points out, the narrator 'hedges his descriptions' with a series of adverbs and, as various ambiguities creep into his account, even begins to contradict himself: for instance, in the first paragraph of the text, quoted above, the dimensions of the cylinder are in 'harmony', but by the eleventh paragraph they run amok (Cohn, 2005, 313). These contradictions multiply to the point that it becomes apparent that something is escaping his account, even if we cannot name or identify that something. The textual construction of the world and its system, which seems to be the means and end of the narrative, ultimately proves incoherent and incomplete, suggesting that something tenaciously resistant, something unformed, remains beyond the margins of the form itself.

The minimalist set designs of Beckett's drama in the 1970s and 1980s have a similar concentrating effect, stripping away social, cultural and historical detail, even as they place a sharp focus on the everyday concerns of routine, habit and alienation. The stark tableau vivant of *Rockaby*, presenting the image of a woman, W, in her rocking chair under subdued light with the 'rest of stage dark', focuses attention on the repetitions of her movements and the recorded voice that addresses her (Beckett, 1986, 433). The lighting, becoming more and more subdued as the play progresses, indicates the fading out of both her life and her confined world, where she has been isolated in her final hours. Standing in negative relation to any recognisable social reality, this unhomely setting defamiliarises the mundane everyday activities taking place within it and (quite literally) obliges us to see them in a different light. It also visually emphasises W's complete detachment from familial care, social relations, affective labour, or any meaningful form of connection with the world beyond her rocking chair and her internal monologue. The repetitive tape-recorded monologue that accompanies W's rocking is divided into four sections, each with a limited range of statements, which at times echo lines from earlier sections, while at other times adding new material to create patterns of iteration and variation. In this way, the play creates a sense of permutation, rather than a rising and falling arc of action. These repetitions-towards-death have often been read in Existentialist or quasi-Existentialist terms as a commentary on the relentlessness of time, the inevitability of repetition, the inescapability of solitude, or the ultimate isolation of human mortality. Coming in the closing lines of the play, the startling phrase 'fuck life' can be read as a demand to exit this cycle of repetition and to bring the ceaseless rocking to an end (442). But the routinised behaviour and the iterative voice also speak to the concerns of the everyday, as announced in the repeated line 'Till in the end / the day came / in the end came / close of a long day' (435). We might then see the image on stage not as a metaphor for the human condition per se but as an image of something more difficult to judge, perhaps something entirely incomprehensible, in quotidian experience.

It bears emphasising that *Rockaby* is not an entirely abstracted or disembodied meditation on the diminuendos of repetition and mortality. Despite her minimalist surroundings, the figure on stage is clearly gendered female, through costuming and address, and she engages in an activity closely associated with the ageing body. The image of an elderly woman in a rocking chair, familiar in Western art and literature, is also closely associated with the routines of domestic life. Rocking in a chair is a custom that is deeply rooted in certain cultural contexts, which assign the activity to periods of resting, relaxing and whiling away the time at an age when economic productivity in capitalist societies is no longer possible. We have seen that a rocking chair also features prominently in the story of young Murphy, as a means to retreat from the big world of social and economic exchange: 'First it gave his body pleasure, it appeased his body. Then it set him free in his mind' (Beckett, 2009a, 6). But, of course, rocking chairs are often associated with the other end of the life course precisely because they offer comfort and relaxation to ageing bodies and can facilitate the process of falling asleep.[15] In *Rockaby*, the chair binds W to the quotidian rhythms that have defined her declining years, even as it seems to ease her closer and closer to death. It is not a mere abstraction then but a familiar, humanised object, charged with emotional association and bearing a certain affective quality, its '*rounded inward curving arms*' suggesting an '*embrace*', as

---

[15] For a discussion of the rocking chairs featured across Beckett's oeuvre, see Bates (2017, 107–9).

Beckett's stage directions tell us (433). Lit with a spotlight on an otherwise darkened stage, the vision of a woman in her chair thus suggests the fundamental importance of such everyday activities, which cannot be dismissed as mere background, insignificant distraction, or some negligible facet of human experience.

Adorno called *Endgame* the 'true gerontology' because the remarkable image of Nagg and Nell in their trashcans made literal the neglect and disposal of the elderly in late capitalist society: 'By the criterion of socially useful labour, which they are no longer capable of, the old people are superfluous and should be tossed aside' (Adorno, 1991, 259). Rocking in her chair, the 'prematurely old' (from a life of overwork and deprivation?) W with her 'unkempt grey hair' provides another emblem of a gerontology that, despite the promises of the welfare state to care for the elderly, paradoxically reinforces their exclusion from society (Beckett, 1986, 433). The utter isolation of W on stage and the projection of the voice of her inner monologue, V, reinforce this sense that she has no value in a world that values people only when they can work productively. Read in this light, the lines that follow the opening suggest her internalisation of these value judgements and the worth they attribute to her everyday life: 'when she said / to herself / whom else / time she stopped / *time she stopped* / going to and fro / all eyes / all sides / high and low / for another like herself / another creature like herself / a little like / going to and fro' (435). Reiterations and rearrangements of these lines appear throughout the entirety of the play. Spending her days rocking in her chair, W maintains a repetitive activity akin to the routines of domestic, or even factory, labour, but this is not socially productive labour. This is only emphasised by the fact that the chair is 'controlled mechanically without assistance from W', so that she appears as a passive body along for the ride, rather than an autonomous agent controlling her own activity (434).

Rockaby also dramatises the all-but-ceaseless interpellation of the late capitalist subject – a kind of internalised terrorism of self-inflicted repression. The externalised voice observes W's behaviour in the third person and calls for an end to her unproductive activity; at the same time, it approximates W's perspective, as she observes 'another creature like herself', who should give up her repetitive behaviour (Beckett, 1986, 435). This observation, like the eyes that observe her on 'all sides / high and low', announces the judgement of others, of social conscience, on her behaviour. But, as we have seen in other examples of Beckett's drama, the play does not let the audience off so lightly from its role in this oppressive arrangement. The eyes mentioned in the text also belong to spectators in the theatre, who again become complicit in a system of judgements that relegates socially unproductive behaviour to marginalisation and isolation, while nonetheless making W an object of close inspection. Indeed, to the degree that the prolonged repetition and minimal variation of the play might lead the audience to feel that 'it is time she stopped', they have been implicated in the same ideological positioning that would devalue the everyday life of the elderly and wish for its final termination (435). Seen in this light, W presents us with an image of what has become of human beings under the conditions of modernity, positioned against a thoroughly impoverished background that, in its negativity, asks us to contemplate and critique something in everyday life that we might overlook too readily in our social reality.

Conclusion

Beckett's most compact theatre piece, *Breath*, is arguably his most concrete, grounded in a world that has become nothing but refuse: as the curtain rises, a 'faint light' illuminates a 'stage littered with rubbish ... no verticals, all lying' (Beckett, 1986, 371). This intermedial 'play' presents us with this scene for a total of thirty-five seconds, as the light increases and we hear a brief cry followed immediately by an inspiration and then, after a brief hold and silence, a slow decrease of light and expiration, until another brief hold and the descent of the curtain. The scene is material, visceral, made up of discarded objects, but it is also detached from any explicit social or political context and any established symbolic meaning. There are no actors or 'characters', no discernible lines of 'dialogue', only the most minimal 'plot', if the inhalation, exhalation and pause can be conceived of as a plot. Instead, in its radical minimalism, it offers a heterotopian 'setting', displaying the material consequences of consumer culture, which produces waste at virtually the same rate that it produces new products for its consumers. The life cycle of these products is linked to the human life cycle by the voiceover 'breath', which stands metonymically for a lifetime of getting and spending, consuming and casting off, day after day as we inch towards the grave (perhaps pausing momentarily, like Nagg and Nell, to occupy our own place in the ashbins, before we fulfil our fates; or like Murphy, to have our cremated remains scattered in the sawdust on a pub floor, ashes to ashes, dust to dust). In one sense, the play offers a brief existential allegory about the ephemeral nature of human life and the ultimate destination of us all, regardless of our ambitions or pretensions. But the composition and production of the piece in the late 1960s suggest a more specific set of associations with the dissatisfactions, the strictures and the terrorisms of everyday life in late capitalist society.

These associations become more forceful if we view Beckett's brief playlet alongside contemporaneous art movements that employed trash and other found objects to investigate these very concerns. Perhaps the most direct comparison

About the Author

Patrick Bixby is Foundation Professor of Humanities at Arizona State University and former President of the Samuel Beckett Society. His books, which range across the fields of mobility studies, modernist studies, and Irish studies, include *License to Travel: A Cultural History of the Passport*, *Nietzsche and Irish Modernism*, and *Samuel Beckett and the Postcolonial Novel*.

In memoriam Leo Bersani

Sartre, Jean-Paul ([1943] 1956), *Being and Nothingness: An Essay on Phenomenological Ontology*, trans. Hazel E. Barnes, New York: Philosophical Library.

Wade, Geoff (1992), 'Marxism and Modernist Aesthetics', in Stephen Regan (ed.), *The Politics of Pleasure: Aesthetics and Cultural Theory*, London: Open University Press, pp. 109–32.

Whiteley, Gillian (2010), *Junk: Art and the Politics of Trash*, London: Bloomsbury.

Žižek, Slavoj (2019), *Sex and the Failed Absolute*, London: Bloomsbury.

Cary Nelson and Lawrence Grossberg (eds.), *Marxism and the Interpretation of Culture*, Urbana-Champaign, IL: University of Illinois Press, pp. 75–84.

Lefebvre, Henri (1991), *The Production of Space*, trans. Donald Nicholson-Smith, New York: Wiley.

Lefebvre, Henri ([1947, 1961, 1981] 2002), *Critique of Everyday Life: The One-Volume Edition*, London: Verso.

Little, James (2020), *Samuel Beckett in Confinement: The Politics of Closed Space*, London: Bloomsbury.

Lukács, Georg (1963), *The Meaning of Contemporary Realism*, trans. John and Necke Mander, London: Merlin.

Lukács, Georg (1974), *Soul and Form*, trans. Anna Bostock, Cambridge, MA: MIT Press.

Maude, Ulrika (2014), 'Convulsive Aesthetics: Beckett, Chaplin and Charcot', in S. E. Gontarski (ed.), *Edinburgh Companion to Samuel Beckett and the Arts*, Edinburgh: Edinburgh University Press, pp. 44–53.

McNaughton, James (2018), *Samuel Beckett and the Politics of Aftermath*, Oxford: Oxford University Press.

McNaughton, James (2024), 'Rubber Genocide in Joyce and Beckett: From Roger Casement's Congo to Vél d'Hiv and Auschwitz', *Interventions: International Journal of Postcolonial Studies*, 27:1, pp. 1–38.

Morin, Emily (2017), *Beckett's Political Imagination*, Cambridge: Cambridge University Press.

Nixon, Mark (2019), 'Introduction', *Journal of Beckett Studies*, 28:1, pp. 1–4.

Nixon, Mark, and Dirk Van Hulle, eds. (2019), 'Never Neglect the Small Things: Beckett and the Everyday', special issue, *Journal of Beckett Studies*, 28:1.

Olson, Liesl (2014), *Modernism and the Ordinary*, Oxford: Oxford University Press.

Oppenheim, Lois (2000), *The Painted Word: Samuel Beckett's Dialogue with Art*, Ann Arbor, MI: University of Michigan Press.

O'Toole, Fintan (2018), 'Where Lost Bodies Roam', *New York Review of Books*, 7 June, www.nybooks.com/articles/2018/06/07/samuel-beckett-where-lost-bodiesroam/.

Ross, Kristin (1996), *Fast Cars, Clean Bodies: Decolonization and the Reordering of French Culture*, Cambridge, MA: MIT Press.

Ross, Kristin (1997), 'French Quotidian', in Lynn Gumpert (ed.), *The Art of the Everyday: The Quotidian in Postwar French Culture*, New York: New York University Press, pp. 19–30.

Ross, Kristin (2023), *The Politics and Poetics of Everyday Life*, London: Verso.

Cohn, Ruby (2005), *A Beckett Canon*, Ann Arbor, MI: Michigan University Press.

Connor, Steven (2014), *Beckett, Modernism, and the Material Imagination*, Cambridge: Cambridge University Press.

Davies, William (2020), *Samuel Beckett and the Second World War: Politics, Propaganda, and a 'Universal Become Provisional'*, London: Bloomsbury.

de Certeau, Michel (1984), *The Practice of Everyday Life*, trans. Steven Rendell, Berkeley, CA: University of California Press.

Esslin, Martin (1961), *The Theatre of the Absurd*, New York: Anchor Books.

Fehsenfeld, Martha (1987), 'From the Perspective of an Actress/Critic: Ritual Patterns in Beckett's *Happy Days*', in Katherine H. Burkman (ed.), *Myth and Ritual in the Plays of Samuel Beckett*, London: Fairleigh Dickinson University Press, pp. 50–5.

Felski, Rita (2000), 'The Invention of Everyday Life', in *Doing Time: Feminist Theory and Postmodern Culture*, New York: New York University Press, pp. 77–98.

Foucault, Michel (1986), 'Of Other Spaces', *Diacritics*, 16, pp. 22–7.

Gontarski, S. E. (1977), *Beckett's* Happy Days*: A Manuscript Study*, Columbus, OH: Publications Committee, Ohio State University Libraries.

Gontarski, S. E. (1985), *The Intent of Undoing in Samuel Beckett's Dramatic Texts*, Bloomington, IN: Indiana University Press.

Goudouna, Sozita (2018), *Beckett's* Breath*: Anti-theatricality and the Visual Arts*, Edinburgh: Edinburgh University Press.

Harari, Dror (2010), 'Breath and the Tradition of 1960's New Realism: Between Theatre and Art', *Samuel Beckett Today/Aujourd'hui*, 22, pp. 423–33.

Hardt, Michael (1999), 'Affective Labour', *Boundary 2*, 26:2, pp. 89–100.

Heidegger, Martin ([1927] 1962), *Being and Time*, trans. John Macquarrie and Edward Robinson, Oxford: Blackwell.

Kleinberg-Levin, David (2015), *Beckett's Words: The Promise of Happiness in a Time of Mourning*, London: Bloomsbury.

Knowlson, James (1996), *Damned to Fame: The Life of Samuel Beckett*, London: Bloomsbury.

Langbauer, Laurie (2019), *Novels of Everyday Life: The Series in English Fiction, 1850–1930*, Cornell, NY: Cornell University Press.

Lefebvre, Henri (1971), *Everyday Life in the Modern World*, trans. Sacha Rabinovitch, New York: Harper & Row.

Lefebvre, Henri (1987), 'Everyday and Everydayness', *Yale French Studies*, 73, pp. 7–11.

Lefebvre, Henri (1988), 'Toward a Leftist Cultural Politics: Remarks Occasioned by the Centenary of Marx's Death', trans. David Reifman, in

References

Adorno, Theodor (1991), *Notes to Literature*, ed. Rolf Tiedemann, trans. Sherry Weber Nicholsen, New York: Columbia University Press.

Adorno, Theodor (1997), *Aesthetic Theory*, ed. Gretel Adorno and Rolf Tiedemann, trans. Robert Hullot-Kentor, New York: Continuum.

Barthes, Roland (2013), *Mythologies: The Complete Edition, in a New Translation*, trans. Richard Howard and Annette Lavers, New York: Farrar, Straus and Giroux.

Bates, Julie (2017), *Beckett's Art of Salvage: Writing and Material Imagination, 1932–1987*, Cambridge: Cambridge University Press.

Bates, Julie (2019), 'The Political and Aesthetic Power of the Everyday in Beckett's *Happy Days*', *Journal of Beckett Studies*, 28:1, pp. 52–66.

Beckett, Samuel (1957), *Proust*, London: Grove.

Beckett, Samuel (1986), *The Complete Dramatic Works*, London: Faber & Faber.

Beckett, Samuel (1993), *Dream of Fair to Middling Women*, ed. Eoin O'Brien and Edith Fournier, New York: Arcade.

Beckett, Samuel (1995), *The Complete Short Prose, 1929–1989*, ed. S. E. Gontarski, New York: Grove.

Beckett, Samuel ([1938] 2009a), *Murphy*, London: Faber & Faber.

Beckett, Samuel ([1953] 2009b), *Watt*, New York: Grove.

Beckett, Samuel (2011), *The Letters of Samuel Beckett, Vol. II: 1941–1956*, ed. George Craig, Martha Dow Fehsenfeld, Dan Gunn and Lois More Overbeck, Cambridge: Cambridge University Press.

Bersani, Leo, and Ulysse Dutoit (1993), *Arts of Impoverishment: Beckett, Rothko, Resnais*, Cambridge, MA: Harvard University Press.

Bixby, Patrick (2009), *Samuel Beckett and the Postcolonial Novel*, Cambridge: Cambridge University Press.

Blanchot, Maurice (1987), 'Everyday Speech', *Yale French Studies*, 73, pp. 12–20.

Camus, Albert (1955), *The Myth of Sisyphus and Other Essays*, trans. Justin O'Brien, New York: Knopf.

Cavell, Stanley (1976), 'Ending the Waiting Game: A Reading of Beckett's *Endgame*', in *Must We Mean What We Say? A Book of Essays*, Cambridge: Cambridge University Press, pp. 115–63.

Cogle, Jarrad, Lydia Saleh Rofail, N. Cyril Fischer and Vanessa Smith, eds. (2018), *Portable Prose: The Novel and the Everyday*, Lanham, MD: Lexington.

In its negativity, Beckett's writing can begin to show us something about the enduring unfreedom and uneasiness of everyday life in the modern world, more incisively than writing that adheres to a model of realist representation. It would be a mistake, then, to conclude that the fictional spaces created by Beckett, in approaching abstraction or even being brought to some self-referential extreme, abandon all relationship to everyday life. Rather, like 'the mystery of a strange sky or strange room' that he contemplates in *Proust*, these fictional spaces have the capacity to unsettle our habits of perception and thus to produce a 'tense and provisional lucidity', precisely because they disrupt the ontological boundaries that shape our sense of reality (Beckett, 1957, 51). Yet it would also be a mistake to affirm that Beckett's art assumes the power to transform our social and political conditions. Instead, his art is consistently dedicated to dislocating, questioning and even disturbing the real, that which presents itself as semiotically and ontologically stable to affirm the immutability of the human condition and the power relations that depend upon such an ideology. He shows us spare, nearly idealised images of our modern torments, of our contemporary terrorisms, of our social and economic relations, but somewhere in their recesses, just out of reach, another mode of being beckons. If Lefebvre helps us to see the critical capacity of writing that strips away social contexts and constructs heterotopian spaces in their place, he also helps us to identify the potential of works that refuse to describe social reality directly and thus reject the assumption that quotidian existence is something fixed, reified. Extending this rejection to a radical negativity, Beckett's late modernist writing offers a site for critiquing the economic and institutional forces that structure everyday life in the modern world. Ultimately, his art of everyday life does not express or represent the real conditions of historical existence but negates them in a manner that clears the way, at least potentially, for something else.

In this sense, the everyday is defined precisely by its capacity to elude direct representation and regulation, including the efforts of bureaucratic control to codify and manage it, and even the efforts of philosophers and sociologists to make it speak. On the other hand, the refusal of intelligibility in Beckett's writing is entirely consonant with the qualities of the everyday. His writing refuses to assume, as naïve forms of realism do, that the work of art can take full possession of its content. Instead, in dismantling this illusion, his writing repeatedly constructs heterotopian spaces, unfamiliar settings verging on 'worldlessness', that have only the most oblique relationship with empirical social reality. Beckett's art is still deeply political insofar as these spaces deny any utopian vision that entirely overcomes the ever more administered and reified world in which he writes; his writing does not abandon the everyday, nor does it turn away from social reality; rather, it goads us to see, precisely in its negativity, the human toll exacted by modernity.

As we have seen, despite his general reluctance to engage directly with Beckett's writing, Lefebvre does provide a means to understand Beckett's late modernist experiments with form as a proper response to the terrorism of late capitalist society. In *Everyday Life in the Modern World*, Lefebvre claims that, in post-war French writing, language itself becomes the only referent as the author fashions a world, a reality, out of signs that convey only differences and distinctions, similarities and disparities. The disappearance of the referent, according to his 'radical analysis', leads to the dominance of metalanguage, words about words, and thus the abstraction of both content and social context from language (Lefebvre, 1971, 130). The post-war fiction he describes constructs spaces that are purely fictional or symbolic, while denying any certainty regarding the historical positioning of the narrative, though Lefebvre suggests that the stability of such fictional spaces is always subject to the intrusion of temporality. Representation of the everyday is thus divided between the 'real, empirical, practical' and the metaphorical, which, according to Lefebvre, 'tends either towards artificial opposition and illusory contradictions or towards self-destruction in the comedy of insanity' (11). In this regard, he echoes Lukács, who perceives the substitution of an '*angst*-ridden vision of the world for objective reality' in modernist writing as symptomatic of the failure of revolutionary politics and a more general frustration of creative possibilities under the conditions of modernity (Lukács, 1963, 26). But, with his dialectical approach, Lefebvre reserves a place of honour for 'minor' works of literature that address everyday life in 'such a way that it is better not to name it or describe it openly'. If more proper modes of representation have failed to account adequately for everyday life, then these improper forms might succeed in linking the everyday and modernity, in somehow 'naming the unnamable' (Lefebvre, 1971, 133).

developed countries more gets thrown away and at a faster rate than elsewhere in the world: 'In New York, in the promised land of free enterprise, the dustbins are enormous' (Lefebvre, 2002, 337). For Sozita Goudouna, Beckett's decision to fill the stage with scattered rubbish 'is not just an allegorical statement about the human condition as it is often stated, [sic] it is also an ideological and anti-theatrical manifesto that encapsulates a post-war reality' (Goudouna, 2018, 30). Beckett provokes 'a critical historical reflexivity' by depicting the 'singularity and incomprehensibility of the past', even as his playlet remains open to a range of possible interpretations because it elicits these interpretations in 'a critical and historically specific way' (31). For all its abstraction and minimalism, that is, the anti-theatrical form of the play nonetheless generates powerful social implications, even if the historical implications of his late minimalist work often go unheeded. The radically disruptive vision on stage – taken literally, a world made up entirely of trash – constitutes a negative image of consumer society, where everything, both products and persons, ends up discarded. Here is a heterotopian space that constitutes a pithy refusal to affirm any positive content or disalienating message, and yet the brief coming and going of this negativity also presents us with an absence that opens the way to something, anything, else.

In the end, it is precisely this negativity that makes Beckett's art of the everyday so distinctive. To be sure, we might sense that there is a certain negativity inherent in the everyday insofar as it is a domain that is seemingly everywhere and nowhere, obvious and invisible. We cannot see past it, and we refuse to see it. The quotidian is ostensibly the domain of ordinary women and men, their habits and routines, their production and consumption, their relations and emotions, their occupations and preoccupations. But because this domain is so expansive and these activities and affects so varied, the everyday is notoriously difficult to delimit and define. Lefebvre attempts to come to terms with this pervasiveness not by reducing it to particular private or public practices but by registering the repetitive daily rhythms that generally elude our attention and charting the spaces in which our fragmented daily activities take place. Nevertheless, the everyday remains something of an absent presence in his mammoth three-volume *Critique of Everyday Life* to the extent that, as he acknowledges, it 'evades the grip of forms' (Lefebvre, 1971, 182). In his review of the second volume of Lefebvre's study, Blanchot argues that

> The everyday has this essential trait: it allows no hold. It escapes. It belongs to insignificance, and the insignificant is without truth, without reality, without secrets, but perhaps also the site of all possible signification. The everyday escapes. This makes its strangeness – the familiar showing itself (but already dispersing) in the guise of the astonishing. (Blanchot, 1987, 14)

in this regard are the *Poubelles* (trash cans) of the French-born American artist Arman (Armand Pierre Fernandez), who displayed assortments of refuse and other discarded objects in plexiglass cases. Gathered from public dumpsters and personal waste baskets, these small-scale assemblages followed his major 1960 exhibit *Le Plein* ('Full-Up'), which completely filled the Iris Clert Gallery in Paris with trash, so that spectators could only view the 'show' from outside on the sidewalk. 'As a witness to my society', Arman later commented, 'I have always been very much involved in the pseudobiological cycle of production, consumption, and destruction' (qtd in Whiteley, 2010, 112). His work can be viewed as providing a negative image of mass production and consumer society that highlights the detritus inevitably following from production and consumption.

Other artists who deploy the debris of the everyday in their art, including Raymond Hains, Jean Tinguely and the *Nouveaux Réalistes*, could also be summoned to amplify this comparison, as Dror Harari has recently done. Harari positions the work of these artists in relation to the American financial support and cultural influence that transformed French society during the 1950s and led to the emergence of advertising culture and consumerist lifestyles. He further suggests that *Breath* should be considered not just as an example of minimalist experimentation but as a manifestation of 'new theatre' that brings together the plastic arts and theatrical spaces (Harari, 2010, 423–33). In turn, I would again emphasise how, with these means, *Breath* offers a negative image of late capitalism and its consumer culture, which highlights the waste products of consumerism as the representative environment for everyday life. It provides us with a vision of our world at its limit, where the processes of production and consumption will eventually lead, until all we are left with is refuse. This is, in other words, an image of utter aftermath. The stage space, abandoning all the expectations of traditional drama, instead presents us with a scene that inverts and reflects in a radically purified but degraded form the horrors of consumer society. The everyday is what is left over, 'the residual life', as Blanchot comments, 'with which our trash cans and cemeteries are filled: scrap and refuse' (Blanchot, 1987, 13). In this sense, Beckett's theatrical minimalism also brings the function of heterotopian space to a kind of absolute limit, which erodes the boundaries between artwork and everyday life.

The striking tableau of *Breath* condenses the historical problematic of Beckett's late drama and prose into remarkable density. What it offers is unlocatable, even as it is also a vivid image of the irreconcilable surpluses and leavings of the society of consumption and their association with everyday life and human mortality in the modern world. It provides a vivid reminder that this is the outcome of late capitalism: as Lefebvre points out, in economically

Beckett Studies

Dirk Van Hulle
University of Oxford
Dirk Van Hulle is Professor of Bibliography and Modern Book History at the University of Oxford and director of the Centre for Manuscript Genetics at the University of Antwerp.

Mark Nixon
University of Reading
Mark Nixon is Professor of Modern Literature and Beckett Studies at the University of Reading and the Co-Director of the Beckett International Foundation.

About the Series
This series presents cutting-edge research by distinguished and emerging scholars, providing space for the most relevant debates informing Beckett studies as well as neglected aspects of his work. In times of technological development, religious radicalism, unprecedented migration, gender fluidity, environmental and social crisis, Beckett's works find increased resonance. Cambridge Elements in Beckett Studies is a key resource for readers interested in the current state of the field.

Cambridge Elements

Beckett Studies

Elements in the Series

Samuel Beckett and Cultural Nationalism
Shane Weller

Absorption and Theatricality: On Ghost Trio
Conor Carville

Carnivals of Ruin: Beckett, Ireland, and the Festival Form
Trish McTighe

Beckett and Stein
Georgina Nugent

Insufferable: Beckett, Gender and Sexuality
Daniela Caselli

Bad Godots: 'Vladimir Emerges from the Barrel' and Other Interventions
S. E. Gontarski

Beckett and Cioran
Steven Matthews

Beckett and Derrida
James Martell

Pilgrim's Gress: The Beckett Walk
Andre Furlani

Suzanne Dumesnil, Suzanne Beckett
Emilie Morin

Beckett and Leopardi
Peter Boxall, Peter Nicholls

Quotidian Beckett: Art of Everyday Life
Patrick Bixby

A full series listing is available at: www.cambridge.org/eibs

For EU product safety concerns, contact us at Calle de José Abascal, 56–1°,
28003 Madrid, Spain or eugpsr@cambridge.org.

www.ingramcontent.com/pod-product-compliance
Ingram Content Group UK Ltd.
Pitfield, Milton Keynes, MK11 3LW, UK
UKHW021933030226
467659UK00020B/825